Y0-AHR-551

James Hardy Ropes
 from G. F. M.

9 October 1923

THE BIRTH AND GROWTH
OF RELIGION

THE MORSE LECTURES

PUBLISHED BY CHARLES SCRIBNER'S SONS

THE BIRTH AND GROWTH OF RELIGION. By George Foot Moore, D.D., Litt.D., LL.D.

MIND AND CONDUCT. By Henry Rutgers Marshall, L.H.D., D.S.

THE CRITICISM OF THE FOURTH GOSPEL. By William Sanday, D.D., LL.D.

THE PLACE OF CHRIST IN MODERN THEOLOGY. By A. M. Fairbairn, D.D., LL.D.

THE RELIGIONS OF JAPAN. By William Elliot Griffis.

THE WHENCE AND THE WHITHER OF MAN. By Professor John M. Tyler.

THE CHRISTIAN CONQUEST OF ASIA. By John Henry Barrows, D.D.

DEVELOPMENT OF RELIGION AND THOUGHT IN ANCIENT EGYPT. By James Henry Breasted, Ph.D.

THE BIRTH AND GROWTH OF RELIGION

BEING THE MORSE LECTURES OF 1922

BY

GEORGE FOOT MOORE

PROFESSOR OF THE HISTORY OF RELIGION IN HARVARD UNIVERSITY

NEW YORK
CHARLES SCRIBNER'S SONS
1923

COPYRIGHT, 1923, BY
CHARLES SCRIBNER'S SONS

Printed in the United States of America

Published September, 1923

TO MY PUPILS

"I HAVE LEARNED MUCH FROM MY TEACHERS, STILL MORE FROM MY COLLEAGUES, BUT FROM MY PUPILS MORE THAN FROM ALL OF THEM."
—*Rabbi.*

PREFACE

This volume contains eight lectures delivered in Union Theological Seminary in 1922 on the Morse Foundation. In preparing them for the press their original form has been substantially preserved; only that some of the chapters have been expanded, and the whole revised.

What I have tried to do is to set forth, in brief, opinions about the evolution of religion formed in the course of a good many years' occupation with the subject. I have not undertaken to enumerate and describe in any detail the phenomena, much less to discuss general theories or explanatory hypotheses. A reader who desires more particular information on such matters may be referred to the learned, lucid, and judicious *Introduction to the History of Religions*, by Professor Crawford H. Toy (1913: Harvard University Press), or the recent excellent work of Professor E. Washburn Hopkins, of Yale University, *Origin and Evolution of Religion* (Yale University Press, 1923), and to the relevant articles in *The Encyclopædia of Religion and Ethics*.

The first of these has an extensive classified bibliography; The *Encyclopædia* also cites the literature amply. This also I have thought it unnecessary to repeat.

In a book like this, which presents in small compass the outcome of academic lectures that have been worked over and recast many times in the course of twenty-five years, it would be impossible to specify in references my indebtedness to individuals. It will not, I hope, be set down to ingratitude if I acknowledge in this general way my obligation to the many who have collected and digested sources, or discussed the subject from the anthropological or the philosophical side.

CONTENTS

CHAPTER		PAGE
I.	Antecedents and Rudiments	1
II.	Souls and Spirits	21
III.	The Emergence of Gods	43
IV.	Morals and Religion	64
V.	Religions of Higher Civilizations	77
VI.	After Death	105
VII.	Ways of Salvation	128
VIII.	Salvation: Religion and Philosophy	147

THE BIRTH AND GROWTH OF RELIGION

CHAPTER I

ANTECEDENTS AND RUDIMENTS

It is now the prevailing opinion among anthropologists that religion in some form or other is universal. Explorers have indeed frequently brought back accounts of peoples that have no religion at all, but more thorough investigation has not sustained the report. In many cases the error arose from inadequate observation. A traveller, who had perhaps spent but a few weeks with a tribe, did not see anything that he recognized as religious, and hastily inferred that what he had not seen or did not recognize did not exist. Better informed observers have often defined religion in such a way as to exclude the phenomena they described, as when one wrote of a tribe with which he was well acquainted that they had no religion—they worshipped devils. Some anthropologists, again, have drawn the line between magic and religion so as to leave to a large part of the population of the globe only the former. To avoid controversy about definitions we may content ourselves here with saying that no people or tribe has been discovered which has not something that answers for it the purposes of religion, whether we think it respectable enough to be dignified by that name or not.

The testimony of history as far back as it goes is the same. The ancient civilizations, when they emerge on the horizon of our knowledge, possessed religions in a stage for which indefinite centuries of development must be inferred in prehistoric ages over which archæological evidence dimly prolongs our vista. The records of Egypt and of Babylon and Assyria give many glimpses of the religions of the nations with which they came into contact. From Greek historians and geographers we have accounts not only of the religions of the civilized peoples of their times, but of many barbarous tribes in all parts of their world. They nowhere discovered irreligious men.

The antiquity thus in some measure disclosed to us reaches at the utmost to a past of less than ten thousand years, a brief span of time compared with the thousands of centuries in which geologists and biologists now estimate the age of humankind on the earth. The biologist assumes that in the process of evolution the genus which boastfully labels itself *homo sapiens* had anthropoid ancestors who had neither religion nor language. With them we are not concerned. Whether palæolithic man, as archæology discovers him already possessed of various arts, some of which he had brought to high perfection, had also developed a religion is an inquiry into which we cannot enter here. It must suffice to say that existing races on a lower plane of culture have religions whose present state implies long antecedents, and that among the remains of palæolithic culture in some regions objects are preserved which, if they were modern, would unhesitatingly be interpreted as religious.

The universality of religion within the range of our knowledge warrants the inference that it has its origin in a common motive, and the identity of the elementary notions that everywhere go with it implies that they are man's natural response to his environment and experience.

The origin of religion, inaccessible to historical investigation, is therefore to be approached by a psychological inquiry. Our question is, how did men ever come to create religion at all, and why has it persisted, in ever-changing forms, through all the stages of civilization?

If we seek a motive, universal, supreme, perpetual,

it will be found in the impulse to self-preservation.* Spinoza rightly says that the *conatus sese conservandi* is the mainspring and directing principle of all human action. Man has it in common with all other animals, in which it is enregistered in innumerable appropriate instincts. Below the instinctive level it is manifest in protective coloration and other forms of mimicry. Higher up in the scale the instinct is accompanied by a progressive measure of conscious intelligence. Throughout it is the condition of existence for the individual and the species.

Its elementary manifestations are directed to escaping or combating the enemies of life and well-being, and satisfying organic needs such as hunger and sexual appetite; but well-being soon comes to include artificial needs, and the same impulse prompts to the gratification of these. The individual is not, however, exclusively interested in himself, because he does not and cannot exist by himself; his self-preservation is often involved in the preservation of the group of which he is a member. This is very plain in the case of the gregarious animals. In a herd of wild horses or cattle, for example, when threatened by their natural enemies such as wolves, the adult males of the herd surround, for protection,

* I call it impulse, rather than instinct, to emphasize its comprehensive and active character.

the females and the young, and expose themselves to danger and death in defense of the weaker. This is the condition of the survival of the herd, and therefore of all its individual members—the condition ultimately of the perpetuity of the species.

The same thing is true of savages. The defense of the weaker members of the group by the stronger, even at the sacrifice of their own lives, is of course not the result of reflection on what would happen if they should flee from the danger instead of confronting it, but upon an inherited animal instinct. This impulse, which is at first an automatic reaction, is in the progress of society fortified by social motives the antecedents of which may also be found among animals. "None but the brave deserve the fair" is an axiom which plays no inconsiderable part in the mating of many species, and is more consciously operative in the sexual selection of humankind. Both in man and beast it has been a potent factor in the improvement of the stock.

Nor is this group interest manifested solely in the reaction to danger. It shows itself in animals as well as in men in the ceding or acquisition of food by the more capable members of the group for the benefit of the less capable or of the whole community, as is conspicuously exemplified by bees and other insects. The co-operative aspect of the impulse to self-preservation is in man as old, as instinctive, and as imperative, as its individual aspect.

With the growth of man's knowledge of himself and of the world he lives in, self-preservation comes to mean much more than this. There are things in life that are of greater worth in his estimation than life itself; things that alone make life worth living, in comparison with which all lower interests, including life, may appear worthless. And above all worthful things is the worth of self to self—of self in the highest conception of it. Man comes to realize that this is not something given, a native endowment which is merely to be conserved, but that all that is of supreme value is to be achieved through the realization of what in nature is only potential. For the negative, self-preservation, we must then put its positive complement, self-realization, the becoming and achieving of all that it is in human nature to be. With this understanding of its implications and unfoldings we may say that self-preservation is the universal motive in religion.

This corresponds to the experience of religious-minded men and women. An American psychologist a few years ago addressed questions to a considerable number of educated people inquiring what it was that they sought and found in religion, and the substance of the answers in great variety of expression may be summed up in the one desire and aspiration, "Life, more life, a fuller, richer, more satisfying life."

The impulse of self-preservation in itself has nothing religious about it; it is in its lower ranges purely biological. And if man were placed in a world where he was exposed to no strange perils and was unfailingly able to satisfy all his needs and desires, he would find no occasion for religion. The actual world in which the savage lives is, however, very different; he is not secure and he is not self-sufficient. He is beset by perils which menace his well-being and his very existence, and his efforts to satisfy his urgent needs are often frustrated. These experiences may be summarized by saying that something goes wrong with him in a way he does not understand. Thus he learns his dependence, or, as I should prefer to express it, his insufficiency. Let us try to imagine his experience and what it means to him.

Take first what we call accidents. A man is crossing a stream and is swept off his feet by the swollen waters; a bough comes crashing down from a tree he is passing under as if aimed at him; or a rock hurtles down the mountainside directly in his path; a bolt of lightning strikes a near-by tree and perhaps kills a companion at his side; a tornado, like some furious monster, uproots the forest and destroys the rude habitations of men.

The spontaneous apprehension of such an experience cannot be better illustrated than by a passage in a letter of William James's written four days after the California earthquake of 1906, describing his feelings during those eventful minutes:

"Well, when I lay in bed at about half-past five that morning, wide-awake, and the room began to sway, my first thought was, 'Here's Bakewell's earthquake, after all'; and when it went crescendo and reached fortissimo in less than half a minute, and the room was shaken like a rat by a terrier, with the most vicious expression you can possibly imagine, it was to my mind absolutely an *entity* that had been waiting all this time holding back its activity, but at last saying, 'Now, *go* it!' and it was impossible not to conceive it as animated by a will, so vicious was the temper displayed—everything *down,* in the room, that could go down, bureaus, etc., etc., and the shaking so rapid and vehement."*

Then there is the experience of disease. In the midst of health a man is suddenly attacked—as we also say—by an illness; he suffers acute pain without visible or intelligible cause, he alternately shivers with cold and burns with fever. He observes the same thing in others, often terminating

Letters of William James, vol. II, p. 248.

in death. Thus in a thousand ways he is made aware that besides his fellow men, friends or enemies, besides the animals which he pursues or which pursue him, in short, besides the things he is familiar with and more or less understands, there are around him other things that are outside his understanding as they are beyond his foresight or control. These somethings are active; it is in act that man knows them. For this reason we may call them "powers," using that word in the vaguest possible sense and without implying anything about their nature; they are just the "somethings" that do something to him. Naturally the savage's attention, like that of the rest of us, is chiefly attracted by unfavorable occurrences, by the harmful things that the powers do; when everything goes to his satisfaction he does not think about it at all—why should he?

Of these powers man is immediately aware in the acts of which he has experience. It is perhaps not superfluous to say that he does not come to a recognition of the powers by reasoning from effect to cause. The category of cause and effect does not exist in primitive psychology, in which the two are as yet temporally and logically simultaneous, and hence he cannot be led into inquiry concerning the causes of what befalls him. Equally foreign to his thinking is what we call "accident." Nothing merely "happens"; it is *done* by somebody or something.

In his notion about the powers there is one other immediate element, namely, that when something does something to him it means to do it. This again is not a result of even the most rudimentary reasoning. He just knows that whatever does anything does it because it wants to, like himself and other men, and like the animals, which obviously act in the same way.

Psychologists call this the "personifying apperception," and define it in technical language which I need not repeat here. In short and simple it means that man as the subject of experience projects himself and the emotions which the experience arouses into the object of experience. In this sense and limitation it may be said that man from the beginning necessarily assumes the personality of the powers with which he is concerned, but we must not enrich his notion of personality from our own; it means, let me repeat, that things do things because they want to.

The phenomenon is misinterpreted when it is said that primitive man believes that all objects are alive. The savage, if he thinks about it at all, probably attributes life to all objects that seem to move of themselves, as, for that matter, the fathers of philosophy did long after. In generalizations about the universality of life the savage has no interest whatever. The modern child who kicks or beats a stool over which he has stumbled does not do it because he confuses animate and inanimate objects; his instinctive and unreflecting reaction is that it meant to hurt him, and he retaliates its attack upon him in a way from which we draw the erroneous inference that he imagines it to be alive. When a man trips on a rocking-chair in the dark and damns it, it is not because he attributes to it an immortal soul which he consigns to eternal perdition; it is what he would say to a man who on purpose had put out his foot to break his shins or give him a fall. He knows a great deal better when he *thinks;* but the point is exactly that under the circumstances he reverts to the conduct of his unthinking ancestor. All that can rightly be said is that there is no object in the savage's world that is by nature incapable of doing things, and that whatever does anything means to do it.

Attention has recently been directed to the fact that peoples in widely separated parts of the world attribute every kind of success a man may have in his enterprises, and every power or excellence he may have, to his possession in superior measure of an occult force which accomplishes everything that seems to transcend the ordinary power of men or the usual course of nature. Anthropologists commonly call this force *mana*, the name under which Codrington described it in his *Melanesians*. Similar beliefs have been noted elsewhere, especially among some American Indians, and in Madagascar, and the effort has been made to extract from them collectively the "scientific" meaning of *mana*—whatever that may mean—and to base upon it far-reaching theories of magic and religion. The Melanesian *mana*, according to Codrington, is impersonal, and may be lodged in inanimate objects as well as in animals or human beings. It is believed to originate with personal beings, and is possessed and imparted "by disembodied souls or supernatural beings." Practical religion consists in getting possession of this force for oneself and using it for one's own advantage; to this end offerings and prayers are directed. It is morally indifferent and can be employed for the malevolent purposes of the black art.

The adherents of the preanimistic hypothesis are, I think, quite right in their contention that animism is not, as Tylor and his followers supposed, a primitive phenomenon, but the product of a somewhat advanced stage of savage psychology. But whether the general notion of an occult force that has all kinds of efficacy is primitive is another question. However vague man's notions about the powers may be, and however little of distinct individuality he may attribute to them, the experience through which he becomes aware of them at all is always of a particular act at a particular time and place and of a particular character, and it may reasonably be assumed that this particularity transfers itself in his mind to a particular *it* that did it. It may further be observed that the peoples from whom such notions have been reported are far from being on the lowest plane of culture, but are, on the contrary, well advanced in the animistic stage.

Man's reaction to the attacks of the powers is the same as to those of tangible foes. The fact that he is attacked arouses not only apprehension for his safety but the instinctive pugnacity with which nature has physiologically equipped him for such emergencies, all the more when the competing instinct of flight promises nothing. What he does, also, is what he does in like case to repel enemies of flesh and blood. We can, indeed, observe these actions only among existing peoples who have long since come to imagine such powers as spirits; but in many cases this conception of the nature of the powers has not affected the things men do about it. In some parts of the world, for example, a threatening storm is actually fought with weapons and all the gestures and uproar of battle; and doubtless the forefathers did just so before they had any notion of a demon of the storm which they were putting to rout. Similarly the means employed in China to fight off an eclipse of the sun are in all probability far older than the mythical explanation of the eclipse as the attempt of a dragon to devour the sun. The same assumption may be made of many of the things men do when the rain upon which their wellbeing depends seems to be held up. Thus in a village in Livonia, almost in our own time, three men climbed a fir-tree; one made thunder by pounding a cask, one struck two firebrands together and made lightning of the sparks, and the third, with a bunch of twigs sprinkled water from a vessel all around, thus making rain. Much in fact of what is inexactly called mimetic magic is a survival of this primitive stage in which men really worked nature themselves, or started it working, with no second thought about spirits or gods.

If the things thus instinctively done were effective, as they often seemed to be, they would be repeated on like occasions more consciously and with increasing confidence, and the method would be handed on from one generation to another. The successful procedures which in animals in long course of time become organically registered in instincts, among men are preserved in conscious recollection and are fixed in custom.

An important condition of all this was that the powers with which man had to deal were not remote. It was only as present in the act and moment that man was aware of them or had any concern about them; and man could act upon them as immediately as they upon him. They were not supernatural. To men who have no idea of the regularity of nature, of forces and laws, or even of causality, nothing is natural in our sense, and consequently nothing supernatural. They know only the ordinary and the extraordinary in various degrees, with a suggestion of the occult. The powers are, in fact, the only activities of the nature they know. Nor are their doings either incomprehensible or irresistible: when they attack man he combats them and often proves himself a match for them; when they will not work he makes them. That men, or at least some men, can control the powers and use them for beneficent or malevolent ends is a universal belief, the common postulate of magic and religion.

We have thus far talked about religion without defining it. Before we go farther it will be well to agree upon what we shall henceforth understand by the term. Of formal definitions of religion there is

16 THE BIRTH AND GROWTH OF RELIGION

no lack, but I doubt if we should be any the wiser for enumerating and discussing them here. What many of them give is the *idea* of religion as conceived in the author's philosophy, often in sublime disregard of concrete realities; others, trying to find a generic description applicable to all religions, offer something like a circle whose circumference is everywhere and its centre nowhere. The fact that religion is so complex and so infinitely diverse that it cannot be formally defined does not, however, prevent us from recognizing it wherever it is found, and instead of attempting to define it, we may more profitably ask what are the marks by which it is recognized.

In our hypothetical analysis, we have supposed our primitive religious subject to be aware in his experience of something that does something to him; like himself these somethings mean to do what they do; and, prompted by the instinct of self-preservation, he, on his part does something to defend himself or to make them do what he wants. For these somethings we have used the vague word "powers," meaning only things that do things, and presuming nothing about their nature. If now we survey the phenomena of religions that are accessible to our observation, we shall find these corresponding marks.

ANTECEDENTS AND RUDIMENTS 17

1. Man believes that there are powers, however conceived, upon whose behavior toward him his well-being is in manifold ways dependent.

2. He believes that these powers are actuated by motives like his own, and therefore comprehensible.

3. He believes that it is possible for men, in some way or other, to work upon the powers so as to keep them from doing harm or make them serve him.

4. And, finally, he acts on this belief.

That men thus *act* is an essential part of these marks of religion. Beliefs about the powers themselves do not constitute religion; they are concomitants of those human activities in which religion as a practical concern of man consists, in distinction from the disinterested endeavor to understand and explain the world and its working which is characteristic of philosophy and science. There is no religion where man does not do something about it, even if that something be, as in some of the more advanced Oriental religions, the most concentrated doing nothing.

What man does, and what gives its character to his religion, is determined by two factors: What he wants of the powers, and what he thinks about them; and what he thinks about them is, in religion, chiefly determined by what he wants of them. So long as man feels no needs that could not be satisfied by an abundance of material good things and his animal ability to enjoy them—life, health, wealth, power, and pleasure—his gods will be purveyors of such things in this world or a continuation of it; and his practical religion will be appropriate means to get plenty of them from the powers which dispense them. The larger his wants, the greater the gods become from whom he seeks the satisfaction of them.

When, by a radical transvaluation of values, men come to regard these natural goods as worthless in comparison with the worth of a transcendental self, they seek in religion the realization of all the potentialities of this self, and conceive a metaphysical Overself, oneness or sameness with which is the goal of the finite self, its perfection and its eternal bliss. In this sole Reality, now become the *end* of man's desire and not a means to its attainment, the manifold powers of his earlier notions are merged in the Absolute One. From one extreme to the other there is a correlation between what man wants and what he thinks about the beings or Being of—or in— which he seeks the satisfaction of his wants. The relation is reciprocal, but in religion, I repeat, the precedence is on the side of man's wants. This is the path along which religion advances from stage to stage in the progress of civilization, of which, on the other hand, it is one of the most potent factors.

In this advance the elementary notions about the powers which we have taken as marks of religion undergo great changes, and corresponding changes follow in the things men do to get what they want. The tenacity of custom however—nowhere greater than in this sphere—makes it easier to adopt new means of influencing the powers than to drop old ones, so that highly evolved rituals are often an incongruous conglomerate in which all previous stages are sacredly perpetuated.

Against the universality of our four marks it may perhaps be objected that primitive Buddhism, and some other contemporary and cognate Indian religions, acknowledge no power whose aid man can enlist to deliver him from the endless round of rebirth under the inexorable law of the deed and its fruit; he alone can be his own deliverer and by his own effort attain release in Nirvana. The answer is that they lodge in man the power to emancipate himself from the bondage of empirical humanity and the cycle of mundane existences. In this respect primitive Buddhism is in accord with the great philosophical salvations of India before and after it, monist or dualist. In time, however, and with its spread in many lands, it became the religion of multitudes who brought over into the religion they adopted all they thought worth keeping of their earlier religion—gods (renamed), demons, rites, and observances—and did not fail to acquire in diverse ways the outward marks of religion in the recognition of multitudinous powers to whom men turned not only for protection against evils and for help in bodily needs, but for enlightenment. Its Bodhisattvas became in effect gracious gods, and eventually, in the Pure Land sects, authors of salvation, a development closely parallel to that of Hinduism and probably not independent of it; while what may perhaps not inappropriately be called the agnostic philosophy of Buddha was superseded in a great part of the Buddhist world by imposing metaphysical and psychological systems, and the salvation of the individual saint by the aspiration to be a savior to all beings.

Our next task will be to show what men first imagined the powers to be like, and what they did in consequence of those notions.

CHAPTER II

SOULS AND SPIRITS

THE innumerable powers with which man has to do are differentiated in the first instance by the spheres or localities in which they are active; for example, in forest, stream, or spring; in the sky, in cloud and storm, or upon the mountains which gather and seem to make the storm. Or they are distinguished by the things they do, as when a man is attacked by fever, headache, or wasting sickness. The latter class exist only in the mischief they do, so that they seem always to be hostile to men; while the powers which are operative in external nature, though capricious, incalculable, and often violently angry, are not constantly unfriendly; most of the time they are indifferent, and so far as they serve men's needs may come to be thought of as friendly and helpful powers. A fixed division of the powers into good and bad, however, even in the sense of friendly or hostile, is only made at a much later stage.

Such vague notions of powers that do what they do with meaning and purpose, and are only in this sense personal, have seldom, if ever, survived into the field of our observation. Very early and almost universally men began to imagine more distinctly what the powers are like, and therewith religion passed into a stage with which we are abundantly acquainted in all parts of the world and all periods of history. In this stage the powers are imagined as spirits, that is, ordinarily invisible and intangible but substantial and energetic beings, which may be lodged in particular objects, as, for example, in a tree, a rock, a mountain, a river, or the sun, moon, and stars, or again in a man; or may wander about freely without such abiding localization, or at least without any that men discover.

The way in which such notions arise has often been analyzed. They are the product of the man's first adventures in psychology. It is his own nature as he thus discovers it which he naïvely projects into external nature. Of the experiences which give him the idea of soul the most important are, first, the observation of death, and, second, dreams, waking visions, and abnormal psychical phenomena. To begin with the former, a man who yesterday was in full vigor, to-day lies cold, speechless, and motionless upon the ground. It is plain that something is missing. Something has gone out of him— the very thing that made him a *living* man; his *life* has left him. Men have actually seen or heard it go out with the last breath, or in the blood streaming from a mortal wound. That such is the origin of the notion of soul often appears in the very name, which in many widely remote languages is the word for "breath," and in the common belief that the soul is the blood or has its seat in the blood.

The soul, then, was the power that breathed and pulsed and moved in man, that thought and spoke and loved and hated. It had gone out; but whithersoever it had gone it was still the life it was. That it ceased to exist is unimaginable, which is the same as saying that to the savage it is unthinkable. Extinction is in fact an enormous abstraction. Our science may teach us to conceive of life as a delicate balance of biochemical functions which come to an end when the balance is upset; but so long as soul is conceived in any sense as an entity distinct from the body, and as in fact what thinks and feels and wills, and moves the body, there is no reason why it should die with the body.

What manner of thing the soul is, men learned chiefly from dreams. In a dream a man sees and holds friendly or hostile converse with living men whom, when he awakes, he knows to be far away. His soul must have temporarily left his body where it was lying and instantaneously transported itself to a distant place. Such temporary absence of the soul is recognized also in fainting or other forms of unconsciousness. At other times men from remote places appear to him in his own habitat. He recognizes them, talks with them, maybe quarrels with them or fights with them. Their souls have left the bodies far away and come to visit him. He has similar dreams about animals; he hunts them, successfully or unsuccessfully, or he is attacked by wild beasts; that is, by their souls.

The objects which appear to him in his dreams are in form and act exactly like their corporeal selves. These dream experiences, we must remember, are as real as any in man's waking life; they are experiences of sense, and man no more doubts them than he does the evidences of his waking senses. From them he gets the notion that the soul of man or beast is a double of the body, visible in dreams and in waking visions, though ordinarily it cannot be seen. It is generally impalpable also—when Odysseus tried to embrace the shade of his mother she flitted from his arms like a shadow or a dream. If man should ask himself what stuff souls are made of, the thing that naturally suggests itself is something like the atmosphere; and this, in fact, is the common notion of the soul, it is spirit (that is, breath or wind), a highly attenuated form of matter like air or vapor.

It is not living men only who thus in the real experience of dreams are seen, temporarily detached from their bodies; dead men also appear in the perfect semblance of their living selves, and they behave just as they did in life. Here again man has the indubitable evidence of his senses that the souls which have been separated from their bodies in death continue to exist, and to be, except for solidity, just such as they were before. Indeed, in nightmares he sometimes finds that they are not lacking in solidity; they are capable of what modern mediums call "materialization," and grapple with a man and strangle him with superhuman strength. Of such elements the notions of souls are formed, a social composite of many individual experiences told by each to others, and making a traditional ghost lore.

However men may imagine the physical constitution of souls and their manifestations, the far more important thing is that the soul is conceived as the real identical self of a man, and from being so after death it comes to be so in life.

Of the reality of surviving souls, man can have no doubt, nor has he any question that he knows what they are like. The conditions of their existence he cannot imagine otherwise than after the likeness of their bodily existence. The soul as a double of the body is not easily dissociated in imagination from the body; it is consequently believed to linger about the place where the body lies; in uncanny hours it is often seen there. Frequently its existence, or at least its well-being, is believed to be dependent on the preservation of the body, about which the survivors then take much pains. The souls of the unburied or neglected dead are almost universally believed to have a worse lot wherever they go.

Souls have the same needs as living men, and hence at the burial, and often at intervals thereafter, food and drink are provided for them. Weapons, tools and utensils, domestic furniture, are deposited in the tomb; wives and slaves are buried with the great of this world to accompany and serve them in the ghostly state. But though thus closely associated with the body after death as in life, souls are not confined to the body or to the tomb, otherwise men would not see them elsewhere in dreams.

Animals, trees, streams, fountains, clouds, sun, moon, and stars—things that move of themselves and consequently seem to be alive, also have souls; as in living man, it is the soul in them which lives and acts. It is, however, an erroneous extension of these notions about souls in natural objects when it is said that the savage thinks that there is a soul in everything. As I have remarked in another connection, the savage has no disposition to generalize about "everything"; his interest is confined to the particular things that concern him.

Besides the spirits which are thus ordinarily lodged in bodies of one kind or another, and which we may for that reason call souls, there are many which have no such embodiment. The powers of whose doings man has experience in the ailments which come and go so mysteriously are imagined as spirits, invisible somethings that get into a man and do him harm, just as others attack him from outside. It is not impossible that the conception of diseases as invading spirits is in origin independent of the idea of soul. That is, however, a question of no importance for our present purpose.

Between souls and spirits there is no difference in kind, and no boundary. The souls of men and beasts furnish no inconsiderable contingent to the hosts of spirits. In particular it is believed that the souls of the neglected dead become malignant spirits, and avenge their dire fate upon their undutiful kinsfolk or on the whole community. Men who were peculiarly feared in their lifetime become still more terrible after death as evil spirits. On the other hand, ancestral spirits are peculiarly friendly to their own kin, watching over and prospering them; and the spirits of dead chiefs frequently become clan gods, or clan gods are believed to have been ancient chiefs.

When the powers come to be thus imagined after the likeness of souls or spirits, the origin of these notions and their association with man's conception of his own nature lend the powers an increasingly human character, not necessarily in bodily shape, but in thought and feeling and will, and make them more completely personal—the beginning of that anthropomorphic process which is of so great consequence in the progress of religion. The local and functional powers now become individual personal spirits, each of which has its abode in a certain place or object, or is recognized by its specific activities.

This stage in the evolution of religion has since Tylor commonly been called "animism," comprehending in the term notions about both souls and spirits. A more descriptive word for the phenomena, from the religious point of view in distinction from the psychological, would be "demonism," if we could rid ourselves of the evil connotation of "demon" in modern use, and take it in the neutral sense of the Greek *daimon*, to designate spirits good, bad, and indifferent. This terminology would have the advantage of enabling us to set "polydemonism" over against the next superior stage, "polytheism." I shall, however, conform to current usage and call this the animistic stage of religion.

The conception of the powers as spirits has, further, a large effect upon what man does to defend himself against them or to make them serve his end. Two means of making the spirits subservient to man's will are so widely distributed that it is hardly an exaggeration to call them universal. In one of them a spirit is conjured into a human being, who then knows and speaks and acts as the organ of the spirit; in the other, a spirit is introduced into some convenient object and confined there, so that its energies are at the disposal of the owner of the object. These two varieties, far from being mutually exclusive, generally coexist, though one or the other may be more prominent in the religion of a particular people.

The first type may be defined as induced possession. A man who has the gift or the art of getting himself possessed by a spirit over which he has control is called in the books a *Shaman*, a name which is native among certain peoples in Siberia. Other peoples have various names for such a man in their own languages; and considerable variety exists in the methods employed in different parts of the world to bring about the possession, but at the bottom the phenomenon is the same.

30 THE BIRTH AND GROWTH OF RELIGION

Its origin lies doubtless in the mental and nervous disorders which are all the world over believed to be due to demon possession. In a fit of epilepsy, for example, everything in the seizure suggests to the spectator invasion by an invisible power which does what it wills with the subject and in him. It supplants his self-consciousness, and makes his bodily organs instruments of the intruder. In this state his gestures and actions are not his. In Siberia the Shaman himself is frequently an epileptic or afflicted with some milder neurosis, and the practice of his calling aggravates these predispositions, which are further reinforced when, as is the case in some regions, the office runs in families. Such abnormality is, however, by no means universal.

Besides native or acquired susceptibility, the Shaman has to master the traditional art of bringing on trance states and managing spirits, which is passed on by elder experts to their successors. Every Shaman has one or more familiar spirits which he can get into him and avail himself of their superior knowledge and power. He can thus foretell the future, find out what is going on in distant places, discover secrets, detect thieves, and answer all manner of questions for which men resort to a soothsayer or prophet. By virtue of his ability to learn what is pleasing to spirits or gods he frequently gives directions about worship or expiation, assuming the functions of a priest.

Inasmuch as every kind of ill-fortune is ascribed to the machinations of malevolent spirits, it is the business of the Shaman to discover what spirit is doing the mischief and to drive it away. Illness is a spirit that has got into a man and must be expelled. The procedure frequently takes the form of a duel between the Shaman, or rather the spirit he has conjured into himself, and the spirit that has invaded the patient, in which the latter is vanquished and takes flight. We have here in primitive form one of the most widely distributed types of exorcism. The expulsion of disease demons is often accompanied by the use of herbs or roots, emetics or purgatives, for example; of fumigations and manipulations which may in fact have remedial effects; and as these become established concomitants of the exorcism, the Shaman is a forerunner of the physician.

One who has such power over spirits as to expel them from the bodies of their victims must be able, also, to send them into people and make them ill or mad—a common form of witchcraft. The Shaman thus unites in himself many functions which in the progress of civilization become differentiated, and

32 THE BIRTH AND GROWTH OF RELIGION

this fact is an additional indication of the great antiquity, the relative primitiveness, of the phenomenon.

Another way in which men secure control of spirits and make them serviceable to their purposes is by getting them into some object, generally portable, and confining them in it. When Portuguese sailors and traders began to visit the west coast of Africa they found the natives wearing suspended about them small shells or tips of horns sealed up, and rightly inferred that these things were worn for the same reason that they themselves wore amulets—a medallion, for example, or an Agnus Dei, properly blessed—for protection or good luck. Accordingly they called the amulets of the negroes by the name they used for their own, *feitiço*, and the word has passed into other European languages as *fétiche*, "fetish," etc.

The phenomenon and the name were brought into currency by the President de Brosses in a book which otherwise marks an epoch in the study of religions.* De Brosses extended the use of the term, however, to all manner of objects in which a spirit was believed to be lodged, including under it the

Du culte des dieux fétiches, ou parallèle de l'ancienne religion de l'Egypte avec la religion actuelle de Nigritie. 1760.

worship of sacred animals by the ancient Egyptians. Later writers have defined fetishism broadly as the worship of inanimate objects, and some have applied the name even to the worship of the heavenly bodies. In such an extension the term loses all specific meaning, and becomes, as it does for the philosopher Comte, merely a name for the lowest forms of heathenism, with a disrespectful connotation. A famous Phi Beta Kappa oration at Harvard will be remembered, in which the study of Greek was described as "A College Fetish," by which title the author meant only to stigmatize its irrationality and futility. I shall confine my use of the word to the phenomena which it was first employed to describe.

The amulets (fetishes) of the negroes may be natural objects such as pebbles with peculiar markings, the possessors of which are believed thereby to be protected against certain dangers or to be assured of success in certain undertakings. There can be little doubt that the use of such objects and the belief in their effectiveness is earlier than the animistic notion that they are inhabited by a spirit. Upon the latter stage, while the use of natural fetishes continues, the fetish is more commonly a manufactured article, and there are experts who know how to make them for various special purposes.

In West Africa the fetish is frequently a snail shell or the tip of an antelope's horn, filled with a mixture of various substances compounded *secundum artem*. Some of the ingredients are selected on principles of what is called sympathetic magic, as when a claw or some hairs of a leopard are put in an amulet to give the owner courage, or part of a dead man's brain to give cunning, or an eyeball, preferably of a white man, to give preternatural keenness of vision. The reason for the selection frequently escapes our too sophisticated imagination. Chicken dung is a favorite menstruum, with which ashes of herbs or bones, gums, and many other things are combined for each kind of spirit according to a special recipe.

When the maker has thus prepared the receptacle he conjures a proper spirit into it and seals it up with pitch. Inasmuch as the fetishes or the spirits that are lodged in them are generally narrow specialists, a well-provided man will have a large collection of them; one to protect him against this ailment and one for that; one to ward off the evil eye; one to protect him from wild beasts in the forest, or to give him success in the chase; another to make him irresistible in love, and so on, indefinitely. With a less commendable motive fetishes are made also to give the proprietor power over some one else. Into these a hair, a nail-paring, spittle, or—best of all—a drop of the other's blood is put. If this cannot be done, his name will suffice.

The fetish is treated with respect, since the spirit in it might resent being otherwise treated. The owner talks to it, cajoles it, tells it what he wants and expects of it. If it does not work he upbraids it, and if it continues to disappoint him he throws it away—unless he finds a profitable opportunity to dispose of it to a European collector of curios. The fetish maker's explanation of the failure is frequently that the spirit has escaped from its lodging, or that some enemy or ill-wisher has procured a more powerful fetish; in the latter case he may offer, for a suitable remuneration, to fabricate one more powerful still.

Besides these individual and specialized fetishes there are others which belong to the community and are believed to guard the common interests of all. Such a fetish may be hung on the surrounding stockade to keep away intruders, human or demonic, or housed in a little hut where the path enters the village enclosure. It is not only told what the inhabitants want of it, but offerings of plantains or fish or a fowl are made to it—the beginnings of "cultus," that is to say, the cultivation of a spirit which is on the way to grow into a tutelary demon.

The guardian spirit of the village or tribe may be a small oblong stone set up on end or a wooden post, having perhaps a fanciful resemblance to a man. A little assistance from human hands, marking the rude outline of eyes and nose and the mouth in colored earth, begins to transform the fetish into what we call an idol. Idolatry in the proper sense belongs, however, to a more advanced stage in the history of religion than that with which we are now occupied.

The fetish maker must be a man who has control over spirits, and since this kind of control may be exercised through his own familiar spirit, Shaman and fetish maker often come together.

Animals, as we have seen, have souls which, except for their shape, are in savage apprehension altogether like those of men, precisely as in the beast tales of folk-lore or the inventions of modern nature fiction. Man ascribes to them his own feelings and motives; he recognizes in them an intelligence which experience teaches him is frequently more than a match for his own. Some are stronger, some swifter, some more cunning; and it is in no way strange that man should not only try to protect himself against them or to get power over them by charms, but endeavor by more direct means to allay their hostility and make them friendly. Some kinds of animals, especially reptiles, impress men, like the serpent in Eden that was "more subtle than any beast of the field," as peculiarly uncanny. Such creatures seem not only to have souls like the rest but to be demonic species, the embodiment of spirits. Men must very early have done something to make the animals they fed on multiply, and to defend themselves not alone against physical attack but against their more dreaded spirits; and when anything begins that has a semblance of worship, animals get their share of it.

In many parts of the world we find groups of human beings calling themselves by the names of species familiar to them, and frequently regarding themselves as in some way related to the animals of that species. Sometimes they tell a story (myth) about being descended from a primal ancestor of that kind. These phenomena, and the social organization frequently accompanying them, particularly the rule that members of such a group must not marry within the group, have in recent times received a great deal of attention under the name Totemism, and large theories about primitive civilization and religion have been built on this foundation. The American Indians, from one of whose languages the word *totem* is borrowed, and the natives of Australia, have furnished most of the observations upon which these theories are based.

There are, however, other sufficient explanations of the wide prevalence of animal names or of the worship of living animals or animal kinds, and it is unwarranted to infer that wherever they are found they are connected with what is called Totemism. Indeed, one familiar with the origin of myths may be excused for suspecting that when men of a certain clan tell of being kin to a particular species of animal or of being descended from a mythical animal of the species—especially if it is in answer to a European inquirer's leading question—this is quite as likely to be a fictitious explanation of why the clan has an animal name or badge as that this belief is the true origin of the fact.

"Totemism" in any of its manifold definitions is far from being general among existing savages, and it is evidently far from primitive. With the ingenious hypotheses that have been built upon it we need not therefore at this point concern ourselves further.

The doings by which we have supposed that in an earlier stage men defended themselves directly against the attacks of the powers are carried over into the animistic stage, and are then believed to be efficacious in warding off the spirits that mean harm to men; and correspondingly the performances by which men imagined that they set the powers of nature to working for them are now believed to work upon the spirits that are operative in nature, for instance, in bringing rain or multiplying food. One of the results of the conception of the powers as spirits was, as has been already remarked, to make them more like men; and a consequence of this in turn was the belief that the spirits could not only be kept by force from doing harm or constrained to do what men wanted, but that they might be persuaded to abstain from injury or to confer benefits, as men might be in like case. By the side of acts of aversion and constraint, men do things the obvious meaning of which is to please the spirits, to placate them if they seem to be angry, or cultivate their friendship and dispose them to do for man what he wants.

What men do with this intention is the same that they do to a powerful man whose anger they have incurred or whose friendly aid they seek to secure. The universal means in such dealings with their fellows are gifts, of whatever the giver thinks the great man would like most and the suppliant is able to give. Men make similar gifts to the spirits, not because they reason from analogy in the way we have done in our analysis; the correspondence of action follows the conception of itself without conscious reasoning. This is the beginning of offerings, which from this point on play so large a part in religion.

When a man brings a gift to another to appease his anger or to gain a favor of him, it is human nature to make the material gift more acceptable and the request more persuasive by magnifying his greatness, his power, his generosity. And in this combination of petition with praise, which may include the expression of gratitude for favors formerly received, we have the beginning of prayer as the concomitant of offerings. The offering is, however, even in much more advanced religions a *sine qua non*. The principle is explicit in early Hebrew law, where God says, "No man shall see my face empty-handed," that is, no one shall come to a place where God is worshipped without bringing an offering.

The means thus employed to propitiate and persuade spirits we recognize as distinctively religious, and can follow their development and the persistence of the ideas that prompt them through the entire subsequent history. For the means previously described by which men try to work nature directly or by a similar procedure to constrain the spirits to work it for them the word magical is commonly used. Thus we come to the controversial question of the relation between magic and religion. As not infrequently happens in discussions, the difficulty of coming to an understanding often is that the disputants are not talking about the same thing. Neither magic nor religion is a thing that exists in nature and needs only to be specifically described. They are names men give, often very much at random, to a great variety of phenomena; the word magic, in particular, is sometimes very liberally extended to religious rites and ideas which the author wishes to brand as irrational or superstitious. Without attempting to define "magic," which might prove as difficult a task as to define religion, it is convenient to distinguish the two in the way already indicated, and to restrict the word magic, so far as we have occasion to use it, to what men do in the belief that their acts are effective of themselves in working nature, or *coerce* the spirits to do what men want; and to apply the term religion to things men do to *persuade* spirits or gods to protect their worshippers and give them their hearts' desire.

If this distinction be observed, and our hypothesis of the beginnings is sound, magical notions and actions preceded religious; the latter came in in the animistic stage by the side of long-established magical practices, but did not supersede them. Nor has any religion ever succeeded in extirpating magic. Both have the same motive, self-preservation; both seek to achieve this end by influencing the powers on which man is dependent. Many rites even in the higher religions are survivals—sometimes symbolized—of magical performances; and what is of greater moment, acts which in their origin were, by our definition, purely religious, often come to be regarded as so infallibly effective that the element of persuasion recedes, and the rite duly performed is believed, at least by the vulgar, of itself to accomplish the desired result—that is to say, relapses into what we have defined as magic.

CHAPTER III

THE EMERGENCE OF GODS

It has been observed in a former connection that the character of religion in its whole development is determined by two factors: What men want to secure by it from the powers on which they find their welfare dependent, and what they think about the nature of those powers, and that of these factors the priority belongs to the former. To put this in another way—the progress of religion, like man's whole progress in civilization, is the result of growing needs; and between the progress of civilization in general and progress in religion there is not only a parallel but a constant interaction. It is in this way that from among the horde of spirits some rise above the rest and become what, without too great strain on the word, we may call gods. To this process, the evolution of natural polytheism, we now turn.

In the savage state, under conditions where man ordinarily finds himself able to satisfy his elementary wants, his dealings with the powers are chiefly concerned with self-defense against the evils that beset him out of the unknown, and with the multiplication of the animals and plants that furnish his food. Every advancing step in his way of living makes him more dependent on climatic influences. The domestication of animals seems to assure him a regular supply of food in the milk and flesh of his flocks; but the failure of seasonable rainfall is a more serious calamity to a pastoral people than to the savage who lives by hunting or fishing. Men begin, therefore, to observe more closely the recurring seasons of their climate and often to associate them with the appearance and position of certain stars or constellations which are believed to bring rain. The sky itself, in which these phenomena occur, and the sun whose genial warmth makes vegetation flourish or with its pitiless heat burns the pastures and dries up the watering places, are the powers which prosper or undo him. It is not strange that among the hordes of the great Asiatic steppes heaven, that is, the sky itself, early became the greatest god. To this result the fact doubtless contributed that in their wide migrations the heavens and the heavenly bodies alone accompanied them, while gods who had earthly seats were left behind.

That Heaven is the great god of the Mongols and from the earliest times occupied a unique position at the head of the Chinese pantheon is probably to be thus explained. Within the area occupied by the early Aryan peoples also the worship of the sky and the powers of nature which manifest themselves in it was the core of the common Aryan religion, and a similar inference may perhaps be drawn concerning its prehistoric past. Elsewhere the worship of the heavenly bodies seems to have grown up in the agricultural stage.

Under other conditions, where nomadic tribes occupied an oasis or moved back and forth from one pasture ground to another within narrower limits, man's chief dependence was on the local powers which furnished water and food for the flocks. In the animistic stage such spots became the homes or haunts of spirits, to which offerings were brought and petition made. Religious relations were thus established between them and the tribes that frequented their habitat, and they were regarded as bestowers of the fertility of the flocks which was so intimately connected with abundant nourishment, and of other good things. As the proprietors of the place they were invoked to protect their clients from the intrusion of other clans, and, with a natural next step, to prosper them in their own forays. Finally the association with the tribe might become stronger than the connection with the locality, and in migrating to a new region it might take its god along and establish him in a new home.

These examples must suffice to illustrate the variety of development in nomadic religions under diverse circumstances.

When man takes to tilling the soil as a principal means of livelihood he makes himself still more dependent on the forces of nature. If the pasture fails in one spot the shepherd may drive his flocks to another; but the husbandman has no such refuge, and famine may follow a single intemperate season. What makes the transition to agriculture of epoch-making importance in religion, however, is the fact that this transition takes place in climates where the forces of nature—the fertile earth, seasonable rainfall, and the genial warmth of the sun—which make agriculture possible are more constant and beneficent. Man ploughs and sows and tills his fields with reasonable expectation of a harvest, and ordinarily experience justifies the expectation. He comes thus to have greater confidence in the powers that bestow the increase of his labors and to rely on their habitual friendliness, while occasional disappointments keep alive the sense of his dependence. He therefore endeavors to insure the favor of these powers. Every step in the cultivation of the soil is accompanied by a corresponding cultivation of the powers which thus become his most necessary gods. He could not imagine that his labors of themselves would bring him crops without this concomitant. Tilling the soil is not only an art but a religion; from the breaking of the ground to the ingathering of the harvest, religious rites attend every stage.

With these friendly powers the community enters into more regular relations; it establishes in its settlements permanent places of worship and public festivals. Sometimes the nature gods take their place under their own names, sometimes older tribal or local deities assume agricultural functions and are transformed by them. In either case, as gods of the community, they not only give the blessings of nature, but are its protectors and champions and benefactors in all things besides. The things that are done to obtain from these powers fruitful seasons and abundant harvests often have all the appearance of magical ceremonies, and doubtless in their origin were such. But they change their significance, when, from being means of working nature or coercing the spirits that work it, they become part of the cultus of kindly gods, and when men begin to rely on the benevolence of the gods rather than on the inherent efficacy of the rite.

This change of attitude toward the powers is not the only consequence of the transition to agriculture. Under various conditions, of which increasing density of population was probably the most important, cultivation of the soil became the chief occupation and living of the people, and with it came settlement in villages and towns, presently walled for defense against invading nomads or hostile neighbors; and thereupon ensued great changes in the social organization. The oldest high civilizations with which history acquaints us lay in the valley of the Nile, the lower valley of the Euphrates and Tigris, and the valley of the Yellow River in China. In all three the inexhaustible fertility of the alluvial soil and favorable climatic conditions, yielding abundant living with little labor, made it possible for the population to multiply to a point which rendered it necessary to extend the irrigable area or to restrain devastating floods by control of the rivers—engineering undertakings on a scale which could be accomplished only by united effort organized under central authority more permanently in action than the war chiefs of the tribe or the horde.

Communal cultivation was succeeded by private property in land; arts and crafts multiplied; trade and commerce began, and all this demanded laws and an administration of law adapted to far more complex conditions than the customary right of nomadic tribes, while at the same time tribal *mores* lost much of their authority by the fusion of different clans or tribes in a settled population. Towns grew into cities; the city-states were united into larger kingdoms, and eventually into the oldest empires, with greater and more various powers concentrated in the person of the sovereign.

The new political organization was reflected in the conception of the gods, who came to be not merely protectors and benefactors of the people, but divine rulers corresponding to earthly kings. As the human ruler was the voice of the law and the vindicator of rights, so the customs of the community, its common law, and later, as we see, for example, in the code of Hammurabi, its statutory law, came to be regarded as having divine authority and often divine origin. A new relation was thus established between the community and its gods. The public religion became a function of the state, the state an organ of religion. The king acquired a religious character as head of the religion, and was often believed to be himself of divine race. The gods themselves grew steadily greater with the larger and more varied demands upon them in peace and war.

The process, the different stages of which we have been sketching, is of fundamental import for the whole future of religion; for it is by becoming completely human that the gods become moral. The forces of nature as they exhibit themselves in their operations are not moral; no more are the spirits with which the animistic savage identifies them. The initial personification of the spirits only makes their doings seem capricious. They have no *mores;* they do what they like, regardless of all the restraints that keep even the most reckless savage from doing many things he would like to do. It is only by becoming progressively humanized that the gods become morally responsible beings, and eventually ideals of human perfection projected into the divine. Nor is the humanizing of the gods the whole thing; they must learn to take their place in an organized human society, that is to say, they have to be civilized.

To the humanizing and civilizing of the gods two factors principally contribute, worship and myth. A regular and orderly worship requires a place where the worshipper is sure to find the god. Men early believed that in certain places or natural objects they had in some way discovered the presence of a god, to whom they then brought their offerings and made their requests. In other cases they themselves selected some object to be the habitation of the god and invoked him to enter into it and make it his abode, and in the conviction that he is there, offer their worship before it. It makes much less difference than we are apt to think where or in what kind of an object man believes the deity to be lodged

—a mountain, a rock, a tree, an animal, or one of the heavenly bodies; or in a stone or post men have set up for the purpose. Stock-and-stone worship, the rude precursor of idolatry, is often looked down upon as something degraded and degrading. We should do more wisely if we recognized in it a simple-minded attempt to realize the presence of deity—the same motive that leads us to consecrate houses of worship. For in this stage it is not the material object that is worshipped, but the unseen power or the spiritual being in it. The rude stone or post may be roughly shaped into an image, and the archaic idol may be succeeded by a masterpiece of art; the hut that sheltered the village fetish may be replaced by an imposing temple; but this æsthetic evolution does not change the essential idea.

Men believe themselves to have ascertained by experience by what means the favor of the gods is gained or recovered. In the course of time these grow into a considerable body of ritual, and as their efficacy depends on the exactness of the performance, the primitive custodian of the holy place is succeeded by a priesthood, which preserves the tradition and sees that the rites are duly performed. It is of recognized importance also that the community should have means of inquiring the will and purpose of the gods, and the priests often become ministers of the oracle as well as of the cultus.

The constant elements in the cultus of the gods are offering and prayer. The most primitive offerings were probably things to eat, and the belief long persisted that they were really the food of the gods. The resemblance to the provision of food for dead kinsmen or their spirits is obvious, but it does not necessarily follow that the latter was the origin of all like offerings to spirits or gods, any more than it can be proved that all gods were originally ancestral spirits.

The common conception of offerings in this stage is that they are gifts to the gods, though some, such as the sacrifice of firstlings and of the first-fruits of agriculture, which are in fact of different origin, were obligatory, a tribute due to the powers that gave the increase. Many other things precious in the eyes of men are also dedicated to the gods.

Sacrifices, public or private, were often the occasion of sacrificial feasts. On the totemistic theory, the victim was in primitive apprehension the divine animal of the clan from which the offerers imagine themselves to be sprung. By eating together the flesh of their ancestor, the clan draws new life and power from the source, and its members are bound together by the bond of blood kinship. A more

THE EMERGENCE OF GODS

probable explanation is that the food which is offered at the holy place or with religious rites is brought into the sphere of "holiness," and acquires divine virtues, which are imparted to those who eat it, giving health and strength and happiness. The sense of fellowship, not only with one another, but with the deity at whose abode they are gathered, so to speak as guests at his table, is a further consequence. The sacrificial meal had therefore a sacramental character, though not in the totemistic sense, and the participants had a religious experience in the consciousness of the nearness and the friendliness of the god.

Prayer, in both its elements of praise and petition, presumes a personal relation, and in exercise strengthens the feeling of personal intercourse between man and god. This is peculiarly the case in supplication, and in the responsive assurance that the request is granted, which again is a real religious experience. On the other hand, the tendency of early ritual to make of praise and prayer charms potent over the gods themselves—what I have called elsewhere a reversion to the notion of a magical efficacy in a form of words—depersonalizes the relation, and in some religions this consequence has gone very far.

A second factor which conduces to the humanizing of the gods is myth. A myth in the simplest meaning of the word is an explanation of something, an answer to some question, in the form of a story of what happened once upon a time. The oldest myths are in all probability answers to questions about nature which human curiosity early and almost everywhere raised, such as, "What holds the sky up?"—the sky being universally supposed to be a kind of dish cover over the world, with a reservoir of rain-water above it. Or the question may shape itself, "How did the sky get up there?"—that is, for the savage mind, "Who put it up there?" Such Atlas myths are found in many lands. Another common type of myth is an answer to the question why man is mortal—death always seeming to be something unnatural—or, how man failed to attain immortality like the gods. The most familiar example to us is the story of the Garden in Eden, where man, in his reprehensible ambition to be equal to the gods, having eaten of the forbidden tree of knowledge, was driven away from the tree of life whose fruit would have rendered him immortal. Others asked why man is part mortal and part immortal, and answered that he was made of clay mixed with the blood of a god, or that the breath of a god was breathed into an earthen image modelled by the god's hand.

Among races that have imagination and the poetic

gift such rudimentary myths are developed into longer stories embellished with incident and episode, such, for example, as the Maori myth of the elevation of the sky, which tells how the children of heaven and earth finding the quarters too narrow for them while their parents lay locked in close embrace, after much debate and with mighty effort hoisted their father sky aloft, and made room for themselves on mother earth. Many myths poetically represent the sun as voyaging across the sky in a boat or driving a fiery chariot from the east to the west, and may then go on to explain how the sun gets back again every night to his starting-point through the dark north or by an underground tunnel. Myths of this kind, whatever part gods may play in them, are not originally religious, though they may be adopted by religion.

Many myths, again, are explanations of the cultus—how men learned that such and such a god was to be worshipped at a certain place or in a peculiar way; while others, sometimes called culture myths, tell of the origin of agriculture and the arts, how they were first taught by a god, or invented by a man who later became a god.

When once the imagination has taken the gods and their doings for a subject, many myths are created or embellished more out of delight in story-telling than of questionings about nature or religion; but as they attach themselves to the same figures they contribute to the great tissue of mythology. In the myths, the gods, in whatever bodily shape they are imagined, are in thought and feeling and act completely human. Human imagination has no other materials for its kaleidoscopic combinations than fragments of human experience, however it may magnify them, and the doings of the gods as they are told in story are frequently "all too human."

These stories about the gods help men to imagine them as magnified and glorified men and women, with individualities of their own that are not simply the reflection of their spheres of activity. Even the less edifying tales only make the likeness stronger and create a human fellow-feeling. In the progress of civilization such myths became repugnant to more refined taste or a more elevated morality, and objection is made to the scandalous chronicles of the poets in which the gods do all manner of things that would not be tolerated in decent human society. But here again, the very idea that gods should set a good example to men is the last consequence of their complete humanity.

The rise of some of the powers to the superior rank of great gods did not dispossess their humbler colleagues who ruled over particular departments of nature or of human life. Indeed the more numerous needs of men in the progress of civilization tended in the first instance to multiply the powers that presided over them. The greater gods, however, as the gods of the city or the nation, its protectors and benefactors, were more and more frequently appealed to by the community and its individual members in every need; and they thus came to assume a multitude of offices that had earlier been distributed among special functional powers, and to absorb these powers in themselves. The names of these minor spirits often became titles or epithets of the god in whom they lost their identity; and under these specific titles he was appealed to to do the things which had originally been the business of the owner of the name. On the other hand, the name of one or another of the great gods is frequently appropriated by local deities which had previously been designated only by the name of the place or by some local title.

No stage in the development of religion is a breach with its past—even the most radical reform is not such a breach. In natural polytheism the demons who do harm to men in manifold ways keep their old place and are as mischievous as ever. The magical performances that were believed to drive away or expel them or to thwart their malevolent intentions flourish no less than before, and have in fact perpetuated themselves everywhere through all changes of religion to the present time. But in polytheisms such as we are now describing men also invoke the protection of the gods against the machinations of the demons. Sometimes this goes no farther than the introduction into the charm of an appeal to the gods by name; sometimes it takes a more independent and distinctly religious form. Finally it may be taught that the demons have no independent power to work their malice on men, but are only permitted to do so as ministers of vengeance when men have incurred the wrath of the gods. This theory, however, never supplanted in popular belief their independent malevolence.

It is sometimes said that between religion and magic there is from first to last a strong antagonism. This view of the matter follows from a definition of magic in which the antagonism is already contained: natural religion, it is said, is social, its end is the common welfare; magic is antisocial, it is resorted to for ends that are incompatible with the good of society, most commonly to do harm to others. Consequently the community in self-defense tries to root it out and religion treats it as obnoxious to the gods. In the wider sense in which we have used the term, magic may be employed for

THE EMERGENCE OF GODS

social as well as antisocial ends, and enters largely into the rites of religion itself. The distinction between aversive magic, the warding off of demonic assaults on the individual or the group, and productive magic, to multiply the food-supply, on the one side, and mischievous magic on the other, was early made, and persists in the discrimination between the "white," or licit, magic of self-protection and the black art.

To productive magic incidental reference has been made at an earlier point in our inquiry. Such performances as Spencer and Gillen have described among the tribes of Central Australia are of this kind, each group having the art of multiplying a particular species of animal or plant used for food. What may be called corn-dances are believed in many parts of the world to have similar effects on the growth of the crops.

With the domestication of animals, the multiplying power not only for their own kind but for vegetation seemed to be embodied in certain species of eminent procreative ability and propensity such as the bull and the he-goat, and they became gods of pastoral tribes, and eventually of their agricultural successors, who continued to be largely dependent for food on their flocks and herds. In the pastoral stage probably arose the offering of the firstlings, to which later the first-fruits of the soil were added, the underlying notion being that if these were appropriated by men the dam would thereafter be barren or the crops would fail. An excrescence, which so far as the evidence goes occurs only in civilization, is the offering of first-born sons. In the age in which we know them, both firstlings of men and animals were regarded as sacrifices to the gods.

A widely distributed type of fertility magic, which also was eventually taken up into religion, rests on the primitive assumption of what we might call in Stoic phrase the sympathy of nature, more exactly, the identity of the reproductive process in all nature, animal and vegetative. In consequence it was believed that the germination of the seed and abundance of increase could be promoted by the exercise of the generative function by human beings, originally no doubt by the cultivators in their own fields. More or less attenuated survivals of these rites have been perpetuated in several parts of modern Europe.

When an agricultural religion developed, this old automatic fertility magic, which had to begin with nothing to do with spirits or gods, could attach itself to any deity that was believed to give the increase to the husbandman's labors—an earth goddess, for instance, or an astral divinity connected with the germinating season—without regard to the other associations of the god. In Western Asia they were frequently, but by no means exclusively, connected with a great goddess of fertility worshipped under many names.

Town dwellers transferred them, with the rest of their vegetation magic or cultus, to the sacred precincts in the town, where agricultural festivals were celebrated. The effect of detachment from the fields and attachment to a seat of public worship was the loss of their primitive specific significance. This is one—perhaps the oldest—root of sanctuary prostitution, and is probably reflected in many "sacred marriages" and in myths of the intercourse of gods with nymphs or mortals. Other origins need not be discussed here.

These rites appear chiefly in the agricultural stage, and persist in higher religions. They are misinterpreted when they are represented as survivals of the "phallolatry," which some modern writers take for a primitive, or *the* primitive, religion, inspired by the mystery of reproduction. "Primitive" man is near enough a healthy animal not to be a victim of the obsession of sex, which is in fact a degenerative phenomenon of decadent civilization.

Fertility magic of a different kind is one of the origins of human sacrifice. Among the Kandhs in Bengal, for example, a victim bought for the purpose was killed, and the flesh was distributed among the villagers to be planted in their fields. The rites have become assimilated to a sacrifice to an earth goddess, but the primitive part of them appears to be purely magical—the flesh and blood or the ashes put in the ground made the crops grow.

In some barbaric civilizations the slaughter of human victims to promote the abundance of the crops had an exorbitant place in the public religion and was more completely transformed into sacrifice. In Mexico, the designated victim in some cults was treated as a vegetative god, and eventually sacrificed to the sun-god, but this is probably an ultimate development of what was to begin with agricultural magic. In general, human sacrifice in the proper sense of an offering to the gods appears in civilization rather than the savage state, though human piacula are not uncommon, and the slaughter of captives in war to appease the spirits of fallen warriors by a ritualized vengeance is also old. The killing of wives and slaves, attendants and officials, to accompany the dead master or chief to the other world is not properly called sacrifice at all.

Aversive magic survives in many rites which when taken up into religion become piacular. Things which experience, or misinterpretation of experience, taught men to treat as ultradangerous—the proximity of death, for instance—were believed to com-

THE EMERGENCE OF GODS

municate to those who came within their sphere a kind of physical contagion which could be physically removed. In the next stage the effect was attributed to demonic agency, which the same means served to counteract. Finally, contact with such things, as demonic, was believed to render men obnoxious to the gods, and to require expiation. The old performances thus gained a new significance. One widely distributed method of riddance in a great variety of forms is commonly called, from the Old Testament example, "scapegoat rites." The evil, which may be an epidemic ailment such as smallpox, demonic influences, religious guilt, etc., is laden in a boat and let drift down a river or off to sea, or it is transferred to an animal, which is then driven far away, and sometimes killed to keep it from coming back with its ill-omened burden. When the bearer was a human being, the latter fate is often erroneously classed under human sacrifice.

Upon the stage of polytheism religions become vastly more diversified than previously, corresponding to the increasing diversity of civilization as a whole under historical, social, and economic conditions, and the growing individuality of races and peoples. Into this wide field we cannot enter here; it must suffice to have indicated the main directions of development.

CHAPTER IV

MORALS AND RELIGION

At several points in the previous chapters we have touched incidentally on the relations between morals and religion, but the subject is of such importance as to demand a fuller discussion. The words "morals," "morality," "ethics," "ethical," show in their etymology the primitive association of the ideas with the custom of the community. No human society even of the most rudimentary kind could exist without customs, collectively constituting its *mores*, to which all its members are bound to conform, and habitually do conform. In this conformity, and in nothing else, primitive morality consists. Many of their customs have nothing to do with what we call morals, others are so repugnant to our ethics that we stigmatize them as grossly immoral; but by the historical criterion both were moral and as such obligatory. Custom is more than this: to the individual by habit it becomes second nature, and is obeyed with a kind of acquired instinct.

Many of the customs are essential to the well-being of the community and even to its perpetuation, and violation of the *mores* in this sphere excites the resentment of the whole group, the instant reaction of its instinct of self-preservation, which breaks out on the transgressor and may go the length of killing him or expelling him as an outlaw. On the other hand, the whole group feels and manifests its approval of signal fidelity to its *mores*, for example, in the swift and ruthless pursuit of blood vengeance, in bravery in defense or attack, or in the fundamental peaceful virtues of primitive society, generosity, hospitality and the like—in short all behavior conspicuously exemplifying what the *mores* require.

Both resentment and approval have varying degrees of emotional intensity, depending on the deed, the doer, and the circumstances. The important thing is that all members of the group share individually in these feelings, and that the pitch of the common emotion is raised by the contagion of sentiment in the mass and by the common acts in which its indignation or approbation finds an outlet, as when an offender is put to death by stoning in which everybody takes a hand. The enormity of such offense is thus profoundly impressed on all.

If we introduce our familiar categories into this description of rudimentary morality, we shall call "wrong" whatever excites the indignation or resentment of the group as a whole, and what arouses its universal approbation we shall call "right," always understanding "right" and "wrong" for the members of the group and within it.

Conformity to the standards of right and wrong in the sense thus defined is expected of every member of the community, and the conscious response of the individual to this expectation, or his participation in it, is the feeling of "ought," or, as we say, the sense of moral obligation.

In many savage communities certain fundamental articles of the tribal *mores* are inculcated upon the young men when they come to the age to be admitted to the manhood of the tribe, and the rites of initiation are frequently of a terrifying or painful kind, adapted to make an indelible impression on the initiate. Among the Basutos, for example, a severe flogging fixes in memory the injunctions: "Do not steal; do not commit adultery (also an offense against property); honor your parents; obey your chiefs." Some Australian natives enjoin: "Be obedient to your elders; share everything with your friends; live in peace; do not assault girls or married women." Examples of such summaries of morals could easily be multiplied. The second table of the Mosaic decalogue, Thou shalt not kill, thou shalt not commit adultery, thou shalt not steal, will occur to every one. The precepts of Leviticus 19 take a wider range, and include manners, as early morality always does, and as the Latin *mores* testifies.

When a man has done what the *mores* of the community forbid or failed to do what they demand, he experiences its resentment not only outwardly but inwardly; he shares it and turns it upon himself as remorse. In such an experience is the most probable origin of what we call a reproving conscience, as on the other hand man's participation in the social approbation bestowed on him when he has done well is an approving conscience. Again, the anticipation of this experience becomes a moral motive in the prevenient conscience, and ultimately the imperative of moral obligation.

The high level of morals in such points as honesty, trustworthiness, fidelity, among many savage tribes has often been attested, as well as their native good manners, and the deterioration of both in contact with what call themselves higher civilizations is frequently commented on. This does not come about solely because the representatives of civilization are often themselves depraved; well-intentioned missionary enterprise sometimes has a similar effect, the introduction of an alien code of *mores* confusing standards and invalidating sanctions.

The effective operation of tribal morality of the kind we have been dealing with is dependent on the homogeneity of the group and the unanimity and emphasis of its censure or applause. We are most familiar with such a situation in the imperative of social usage. Its unwritten code is purely conventional, neither rational nor moral, and for that reason it is incontrovertible. The feeling we have about an unintentional breach of etiquette is a real remorse and often more poignant than we experience over the commission of an act which is contrary to our moral standards but is easily condoned in our circle. Less than a century ago men of the highest character killed one another in the duel, though the law and the church called it murder, because the code of honor prescribed that remedy for certain wrongs, rather than face the social outlawry that a refusal incurred among gentlemen. We are all acquainted, at least by hearsay, with the professional code of honest gamblers. Such modern instances enable us to understand the coercive power of the *mores* in early society. They admitted no casuistical discussion; their imperative was absolute; the consequence of transgression was outlawry.

This whole development is independent of religion and its premises. Religion did not create the idea of right and wrong nor of moral obligation; it did not generate conscience; nor did it contribute to the content of primitive morality anything but its own customs as part of the general *mores*. The conception of conscience as a kind of transcendental moral law characteristic of human nature as such, by which man intuitively knows what is right and what is wrong, having the authority of a categorical imperative, and armed to punish the transgressor with remorse as a kind of divine judgment within him, is as much a figment as a specific innate religious faculty. The enlarging scope of morals is solely the result of the progress of society in civilization with its more complex relations.

Very early, however, there was given to the savage *mores* an extra-social sanction of immense force. Men on the lowest planes of culture believe not only that by doing certain things they can defend themselves against hostile powers or placate them, and by other means can get the powers to do things for them, but that there are things they must not do on peril of disaster or destruction. There are objects they must not touch, places on which they must not intrude, acts from which they must unconditionally refrain. They have been taught by experience, interpreted by *post hoc propter hoc*, the universal fallacy in the interpretation of experience, that the doing of these things is deadly. A classic example in the books is a story of a negro on the west coast of Africa who broke off a piece of iron from an anchor found on the shore to make a hoe. Next day he suddenly died. Evidently the thing had killed him, and would kill anybody else that meddled with it. A multitude of things in the savage's world seem to be charged with an occult force, a kind of magical electric current, we might say, as mysterious and deadly as the physical kind. The slightest contact with them, intentional or accidental, and even too close proximity to them, suffices to draw the deadly discharge.

The animistic explanation is that a spirit lodged in these objects resents the act as a personal injury; and a step further on the object-spirit may be succeeded by a god to whom the object is sacred. When Uzzah put out his hand to steady the ark of the Lord as the cart threatened to upset, he dropped dead in his tracks, killed by a shock of "holiness," which is the Hebrew name for this deadly fluid. So strong is the belief in the infallibly fatal consequences of such acts that in well-attested instances sound and strong men who have committed them in complete ignorance have lain down and died when they learned what they had done—died because they knew they would!

Persons, things, or acts in which this mysterious fatality lurks are often said to be *tabu*, a Polynesian name said to mean "marked," but now generally used in the sense of "prohibited" by custom or religion. The significance of tabu lies, however, not in the prohibition, which is social and secondary, but in the nature of the sanction, the inevitable, automatic, and incommensurate consequence of violation. The consequence, moreover, is contagious; in the solidarity of primitive society the act of an individual, reckless or accidental, may involve his family or the whole community in his ruin. To forestall this peril the community often purges itself of the contagion by putting to death the perpetrator or banishing him, in one way or the other repudiating all connection with him and his deed.

The notions we have been describing are not moral; but the observance of the interdictions becomes part of the *mores* of the community, and is enforced with the energy of self-preservation. The effectiveness of its double sanction leads men of authority, in the common interest, or for the special benefit of chiefs or priests, to extend the system over large fields in which it had no natural basis. In Hawaii this had gone to such intolerable lengths that in the early years of the nineteenth century the whole structure was done away.

Neither was the tabu originally religious; but the explanation which attributes the consequences of violation to the explosive anger of spirits or gods, provoked by invasion of their domain or by acts abhorrent to them, connects it with religion, where again its scope is widened and its import changed. Eventually whatever belongs peculiarly to gods or is regarded as peculiarly obnoxious to them is put under this sanction. The old methods of physically removing contagion become an antidemonic disinfection, and finally rites of expiation and placation addressed to the gods. The idea of guilt originates in these notions.

Although these restraints on human behavior are not intrinsically moral, many things that were early and most generally interdicted fall in the sphere of morals in our use of the word. The manslayer, for example, even a warrior who has killed an enemy in battle, in many parts of the world requires formal and often protracted expiations or purifications before he can resume his ordinary place in society. Among the ancient Greeks a man who had accidentally killed another had to leave the land for a period and seek purification from a stranger, though he was not regarded as guilty of homicide. The nature of the things done in such cases shows that they were originally means of removing a physical contagion. Savages often give the animistic explanation: they ward off or placate the angry ghosts of the slain. The murder of a clansman, on the other hand, is usually inexpiable in any such way; it demands blood vengeance.

Marriage or extramarital connection between members of mutually interdicted groups—the primitive notion of incest—is also an inexpiable offense. The community may avert the consequences of tolerating such a monstrous violation of the *mores* by putting both parties to death. Elsewhere they are left to reap the consequences themselves. In the Hebrew law, while the adulteress was stoned to death by the whole community, no legal penalty is attached to the numerous varieties of incest. The ominous sentence is, "That person will be cut off from his people"—exterminated by the act of God. The impersonality of the expression suggests a survival of the primitive conception of the automatic deadly effect of the infringement of a sex tabu. It will be found in fact that all the *kerithoth* (thirty-six are enumerated in the Mishnah) are ancient tabus, with divine vengeance substituted for inherent deadliness.

It is perhaps in this way that the gods become the vindicators of certain spheres of morals in distinction from offenses against themselves, or, to put it in a different way, the extra-social sanction of these parts of the *mores* becomes religious. The idea of contagious or hereditary guilt which has so important a place in religion may also be traced to the circle of tabu notions. I need only recall the prominence of this motive in Greek tragedy, as in the fate of Œdipus, or the doom of the house of Atreus.

For the further development it was of great consequence that, in correspondence with the political evolution of society, as was remarked in the preceding chapter, the gods came to be thought of as divine rulers, who, like human rulers in this stage of civilization, become guardians of the customary law of the community in all its branches, and enforce it upon transgressors with something of the public interest that distinguishes punishment from vengeance. They take cognizance particularly of misdeeds that escape detection among men and wrongs done to the defenseless. The divine retribution does not single out morals in our sense for its especial field, but the new sanction it gives is of peculiar significance in this sphere.

As rulers, it is expected of the gods, as of earthly kings, that they give right judgment and execute their sentence impartially. Through this analogy arises the conviction that the gods must be just, which in time makes justice belong to the very idea of God. A good king, moreover, is one who not only thus administers even-handed justice, but who wisely and unselfishly promotes the interests of his people, and this ideal also transfers itself to the gods. A divine tyranny becomes as inconceivable as human tyranny is intolerable. But this belongs to another chapter.

When it came to be believed that the gods were not merely the guardians and vindicators of the customary law of the community, but the authors of all law, social, civil, and religious, every transgression or neglect is an offense against God in the quality of lawgiver as well as ruler, and if wilful is a constructive defiance of his authority which he doubly resents. It is through this immediate reference to God that wrong-doing becomes sin.

That in this way morals acquire the authority and sanction of religion is of the highest consequence, for in the progress of civilization the original authority and sanction are dissolved. They depended, as we have seen, on the homogeneity of a comparatively small group, with simple interests. With the growth of cities and nations of amalgamated population and complex interests, the compulsive force of community opinion relaxed. Advance in knowledge of the world and the workings of nature undermined many primitive beliefs. By taking morals into its sphere and making them part of a divine *law*, religion furnished the only possible substitute for the sanction of the primitive *mores;* a substitute effective so long as the authority of religion itself was not challenged. But, on the other hand, religion, with its characteristic conservatism, gave a degree of fixity to the morals as well as the rituals of the past, the unsorted accumulation of ages. What we regard as moral was inextricably entangled with non-moral interdictions. Misfortune, disease, sin, guilt, punishment, were indiscriminate, and the piacula devised for the one were extended to the other. Religion was not made ethical, but morality religious; and religion thus often interposed a formidable obstacle to moral progress. This is peculiarly the case where the law is fixed in sacred scriptures containing a closed canon of revelation, which admits no addition or subtraction, no change, and thus gives the stamp of finality to the institutions, laws, and moral standards of a past which religion is thus forbidden to outgrow.

CHAPTER V

RELIGIONS OF HIGHER CIVILIZATIONS

As we have seen in a former chapter, polydemonism and polytheism are the universal forms of natural religion when it has reached this level. Man's experience is always of a multiplicity of powers that do something to him or for him, whether he takes it that the things themselves do it, or spirits in the things, or demons that get into him. His multiplying wants lead to a multiplication of the powers from which he seeks their satisfaction, and those on which he relies for his greater and more constant needs outgrow the rest and become gods, without supplanting their humbler colleagues or superseding the more primitive demonism.

At an early stage we find men making gods of the instruments they employ to supply their needs, implements of the chase and weapons of war, the tools of primitive agriculture or the apparatus of primitive arts. Here, as in so many other cases, an original magical efficacy develops into religion. A similar process may be assumed when the apparatus of worship comes to be itself an object of worship—cultus gods, such as Agni, the sacrificial fire, Soma, the libation, in India, which in the Rig Veda take rank with the greatest of the nature-gods.

The development of polytheism does not proceed in isolation, and consequently polytheisms are generally composite. Kindred tribes may confederate or combine in larger groups with an ensuing inclusive association of their gods in the common religion of the amalgamated people; neighboring towns grow together into a city with similar result; the union of petty states in a kingdom brings their gods into a comprehensive national pantheon; the consciousness of racial unity without political union may accomplish the same thing; conquest or colonization not only plants the gods of the conquerors in new regions, but often incorporates the gods of the conquered in the pantheon of the conquerors, a process much facilitated by the identification of the alien gods with those of the newcomers. The religion of the Greeks and the Romans affords familiar examples of all these phenomena as well as of the introduction of strange deities by the ways of commerce and of the deliberate borrowing of gods for particular purposes or emergencies. The process went on on a vastly enlarged scale through the whole extent of Alexander's empire and the Macedonian kingdoms that succeeded it, and in the Roman world ended in a universal syncretism of gods and cults in the whole Mediterranean area, which was, so to speak, the *reductio ad absurdum* of polytheism, and gave an effective argument to the philosophical and religious advocates of the unity of the godhead.

Political progress reflects itself in the world of the gods. The tutelary god of a city which establishes its dominion over other territories, or the national god of a conquering people, often becomes the god of the kingdom or eventually of an empire, as is exemplified in Egypt, where Amon, the ram-god of Thebes, hyphenated with Ra, the solar deity, became the god of the Theban empire, in whose name wars were waged and to whom the largest share of the spoils was dedicated, but without superseding the other gods in their own seats or reducing them at home to a subordinate rank. On the other hand, a great nature-god, like Tien (Heaven) in China, may be the "Supreme Emperor" (Shang-ti) by native right, and be correlated in the state religion to the human emperor, the Son of Heaven.

In early monarchies the king was commonly the religious as well as the civil head of the nation, exercising in person on great occasions priestly functions, some of which were reserved to him alone, while others were deputed by him to the ordinary ministers of the cultus. Conversely, the sacerdotal character of the king made it all the more natural for men to think of the god as a divine king.

With the advance of civilization and the accumulation of wealth, the cultus became more elaborate and more magnificent; the gods bestowed larger gifts on their people, and their worshippers reciprocated in larger gifts to the gods. Where in older times the place of worship was a sacred precinct surrounding the altar under the open sky or a simple fane, temples were now reared, palaces for the deity, which from age to age became greater and more splendid. The treasures of cities and empires were lavished upon them, and they were built and embellished with all the resources of art. The rude stone or post in which the deity was present to receive the homage of his worshippers was succeeded by an image of the god in the likeness of man or beast or the two together, and finally among some peoples, an art was created which expressed their highest conceptions of divinity.

Here, however, wide diversities appear in different religions. What has been said applies eminently to Egypt, Babylonia, and Greece. In China, where the great powers or spirits of nature are worshipped in their proper character under the open sky, the state religion evolved a cultus as splendid and impressive as has ever been seen, without temples or images. In Vedic India, where there were not even permanently sacred precincts, the place of sacrifice being marked off and consecrated for the occasion, no temples were reared, no images fashioned. Jains and Buddhists, with no gods to begin with, created a characteristic religious architecture and a notable art of sculpture in monuments of their founders, and presently in temples housing multitudes of images, and developed a stately cultus, normally without animal sacrifices. The modern religions of India followed with innumerable temples and hosts of grotesque idols.

The fundamental elements of worship continue to be offerings and prayer, but the variety and magnitude of the offerings increase and formulas of prayer for different occasions and circumstances multiply. The success of the rite depends on the exactness of the performance in act and word, which becomes matter of expert knowledge and professional tradition. The priesthoods often grow to be inordinately numerous; they are classified by their special functions, and ranked in a hierarchy. In some countries, as in Egypt, they acquired enormous corporate wealth, and a power which more than once proved a peril or a disaster to the state. The Brahmans in India attained an even greater power without organization and without material means.

In China, at the opposite pole, the whole public cultus was a function of the state, and was performed by the emperor, by vassal princes for their territories, or by the viceroys, governors, and other officials in their several ranks as part of their governmental duty. The necessary expert knowledge of the ritual was furnished by masters of ceremonies who were learned in such matters. There was no professional priesthood at all.

In Greece—to illustrate the diversity by but one other example—the priests of the various temples were in historical times often chosen from the citizen body by lot or election, for life or a term of years. While in service they were subject to certain restrictions and observances, but they had no intrinsic sacerdotal character and formed no priestly class.

This accounts for the fact that the history of religious thought and philosophical speculation in Greece are so completely secular, in the sharpest contrast to ancient India. And indeed henceforward the character and influence of the priesthood are most important factors in the development and diversification of religions. In India philosophical speculation began in Brahman circles, though even in the Upanishads laymen participate in it; then came an anti-Brahmanic movement, best represented for us in Buddhism, which rejected the Vedas with all the pretensions of the priests, seeking other ways of salvation; and finally the modern religions of India, non-Brahmanic in origin however largely Brahmanized in the course of time. In Greece, on the other hand, it was from the first the poets and philosophers who did all the thinking and led the way to higher conceptions of the godhead and what the gods require of men. In Israel, again, the epoch-making steps of progress were made by the prophets and in later times by the scribes, not by the priesthood as such.

In some religions, as in Greece, enrichment and æsthetic refinement of the cultus are carried very far without radical departure from the older model. The softer manners of civilization lead to the attenuation of many savage rites; the slaughter of a human victim in sacrifice or expiation may be reduced to the scratching of the neck with the priest's knife or to a mere gesture. Processions and dances, mimes and plays of a very primitive type are developed into a stately ceremonial, or into a noble drama. From being magical means to work nature or the spirits in nature, they came to be spectacles well-pleasing to the gods, who, being the ideal of cultivated Greeks, were gratified by the things in which their worshippers delighted.

The older notion was that the portion of the sacrifice that was offered to the gods was the food of the gods. For chthonic deities it was buried, or the blood was poured into a pit in the earth; for gods of rivers or of the sea, it was committed to the waters. Etherialized by burning on the altar it ascended to the sky in a savory smoke, which the heavenly gods sniffed with satisfaction. When the gods grew greater, and came to be thought of as the bestowers of all good things on men, the reflection arose that they can be in no need of the paltry gifts men make them out of their share in the great gifts of the gods, and sacrifice and offering assumed for such thinkers the character of homage.

In human society, men bring a present to a king such as is within their ability, and the king, though he has no need of it, accepts it as a token of the loyalty and good-will of the giver. So it is with the gods also. It is not the magnitude and costliness of the offering that count, but the spirit in which it is offered. Where the conviction is reached that the gods are just, and demand of men uprightness and humanity in their dealings with their fellows, the consequence is drawn that they cannot be propitiated or persuaded to condone wrong-doing by the offerings and supplications of the wrong-doer— to imagine that they can is to impute to them the character of bribable judges. The efficacy of sacrifice is thus morally conditioned.

In conflict with such moralizing of the cultus is the powerful and persistent interest of the offerer to be assured of the efficacy of the means and the certainty of the result. It is natural also that priests should believe in the unconditional potency of the propitiatory sacrifices and expiations which they make, and should cultivate this confidence in the minds of their clients. Monstrous misdeeds may demand extraordinary expiations; but somewhere in the arsenal of piacula there must be remedial rites adequate to the worst offenses. Moreover, the worst offenses in the religious point of view were not what we call moral, but acts or neglects which affected the gods directly and constituted religious *læsa maiestas*, while wrongs done to fellow men interested the gods only indirectly and more remotely. It was this natural logic of religion that made the contradictory doctrine in the mouth of the Hebrew prophets sound to their contemporaries not only absurd but godless, and it may be doubted whether the teaching of Plato had greater effect in religion.

The most outspoken assertion of the unconditional efficacy of ritual is in India. The Brahman priest by the ceremonies he performs makes the gods do what the worshipper wants, and he is therefore an earthly god, obviously more powerful than the gods whom he constrains to do his will. This is only the extreme consequence of the interest both priest and worshipper have in guaranteeing the result.

Apart from such extravagant valuation of the cultus, the perpetuation of the ancient forms of expiation of itself hindered the rational and moral progress of religion. Originally physical means of averting by their own operation the automatic consequences of even an unwitting intrusion into the sphere of the ultradangerous, and in the animistic stage antidemonic rites of aversion or riddance, they become means of placating offended gods, and however they may be assimilated to modes of worship and incorporated in the cultus, they are never rid of their primitive magical character.

When religion has reached the idea of sin as an offense against good and just gods, and has thus given a new meaning to morality, the notion that moral guilt can be nullified by physical means is in conflict with all higher religious conceptions. Bolder thinkers like Heraclitus poured their scorn on its absurdity; more conservative souls had recourse to symbolic interpretation, which in all ages is the approved method of reconciling men to irrational and immoral survivals in a religion which they have outgrown. But for the masses ritual expiation remained the easy way to get rid of the consequences of their misdeeds without the painful necessity of reforming their lives.

Mythology, which in earlier times did much to make the gods completely human and thus put them in the way of becoming moral, is another obstacle to the complete moralizing of religion, particularly where it is part of an authoritative priestly tradition, or, as in Greece, has acquired an equivalent authority through the poets. Myths in which operations of nature such as the fertilization of the earth by the sky were imagined as the deeds of man-like deities, become recitals of divine adulteries and incests, which were multiplied by poetic imitations. The genealogies of gods and heroes abound in relations no less contrary to even the rudest morals. The cosmogonic theogonies, as they are told in Hesiod and after, are full of savage crimes. The gods of Homer instigate and promote deeds such as men universally condemn, and are guilty of like crimes themselves.

When men got to the point of conceiving that the gods should be examples of human virtues, they found them in the mythical theology to be examples of all human and superhuman vices. And the worst was, as Plato emphasizes, that the education of youth was based on the poets, and their minds in their most absorbent years were imbued with these examples, made the more harmful by the charm of noble poetry, the prestige of venerable antiquity, and the belief in poetic inspiration. It is no wonder that Greek religion was attacked from this side in the name of religion and morality as well as of reason. Less radical minds, conscious of the incompatibility of the myths with the very idea of godhead, found a way of escape from the dilemma by allegory, as they got over similar difficulties in the cultus by symbolism, and saved themselves from the necessity of rejecting either the myths or the gods by discovering a deeper meaning in the myths that was not only harmless but even enlightening and edifying, as the fathers of the Christian church subsequently did with the Old Testament. But however satisfying these circles may have found their own fictions, such interpretations did not do much to counteract in the general mind the harm that established ritual and accepted mythology wrought.

We have seen in a former connection how the Shaman, or rather the spirit he conjures into himself, gives answers to questions about all sorts of things which there is no natural means of knowing. This is perhaps the oldest form of natural divination and the origin of the idea of revelation. In more advanced religions the inquiries are addressed to gods, as in the oracle at Delphi, where the Pythia went into a frenzy, and her inarticulate ravings, inspired by the god, were interpreted in verse by the prophet of the oracle. Another very ancient and almost universal mode of inquiry of the gods is by the lot, which sometimes becomes an elaborate technique. The gods also of their own motion gave signs to men, omens and portents, which were interpreted by inspired seers or by professional experts.

Another widely distributed mode of divination was the inspection of the inwards of sacrificial victims, favorable or unfavorable responses being drawn from abnormal appearances, particularly in the liver. Practised to-day by wild tribes in Borneo and the Philippines, the extispicia were developed into a complicated procedure by a branch of the Babylonian priesthood, and spread thence to Greece and Italy. Another art, in which also the Babylonians had the pre-eminence, was the observation of the positions and motions of the heavenly bodies, and other celestial phenomena. In the centuries before the Christian era, astrology outranked all other forms of divination, and evolved the theory that the fortunes of men were not only written in their stars but unalterably determined by their stars—an astrological fatalism which did away altogether with the belief in divine providence and human responsibility, and contributed not a little to the decadence of religion.

The idea of divine revelation is not limited to such casual and piecemeal disclosures. In India the poets (Rishis) were inspired to put into hymns the praises of the gods for occasions of sacrifice, and these utterances were preserved and eventually collected for ritual purposes in the Rig Veda. Inspiration was not confined, however, to praises and prayers to the gods, nor did it cease with the Vedic age. The rituals of the Brahmanas, the speculations of the Upanishads, the rules for domestic observance—in short, the whole religious literature and the regulations which governed all human life—were divine revelation. Long preserved by guild and school tradition with many precautions against change, it was ultimately written down, though even then the book was regarded only as an auxiliary to memory or an imperfect surrogate for it.

In Israel the revelation of God to the prophets became the type of divine revelation, and ultimately the whole body of ritual and observance, the civil law, and the moral standards and ideals of the nation were believed to have been revealed at the beginning of the nation's existence through the greatest of the prophets, Moses. The time came when prophetic inspiration ceased, but in its sacred Scripture and the concomitant tradition—equally inspired and divinely authoritative—the Jews had the complete and final revelation of God's character and purpose, and his will for man's whole life.

Most of the religions which have produced a corpus of sacred scriptures belong, however, to the class of soteric, or redemptive, religions, with which we shall have to do hereafter.

Though polytheism is the normal form of natural theism, tendencies toward unification appear comparatively early, and in the higher religions develop in various forms. It is not uncommon to find among peoples far down in the scale of culture the recognition of a god of a different kind from the rest, who is sometimes regarded as the maker of everything. He is commonly thought to be up in the sky, from which eminence he sees all that goes on below, and frequently he is believed to disapprove wrong-doing (departure from the tribal *mores*), and to approve conformity to them as men do. It has been held by some modern writers on the beginnings of religion that such "high gods of low races" represent a stage more primitive than the throngs of spirits, bad and good, with which the animistic savage peoples his world, and the many gods that succeed them—polytheism arises from an earlier and purer kind of religion by a degenerative process. Deterioration is observable in the history of religion as well as progress, but in this instance it does not appear that these superior gods are believed to intervene in sublunary affairs; they are said to disapprove wrongdoing, but they do nothing to make their disapproval felt, and men correspondingly do nothing to deprecate their displeasure or solicit favor. That is, they are not gods in religion at all, and there is no evidence that they ever were more than they are now. It is not difficult to explain the origin of such conceptions without the hypothesis of a primitive natural monotheism; but with that question we are not further concerned.

Others find a precursor of monotheism in what is called henotheism, or more properly kathenotheism. In Vedic hymns, for example, it is not uncommon to find the powers and attributes of all the gods ascribed to the one to whom the hymn is addressed. This is primarily a liturgical phenomenon; the god of whom something is wanted is always made propitious by laudation of his power and generosity, in this case by attributing to him the ability to do everything that the whole pantheon could do. On the next occasion any other god may be extolled in the same fashion. This habit may have contributed at a later stage to the pantheism which absorbs all the gods in one, or in some particular one, a process which is the dissolution of polytheism, not the emergence of monotheism. Historically, kathenotheism has never shown any tendency in that direction, nor has the species of pantheism we have referred to.

In Homer, Zeus is king of gods and men. This epic monarchy is, however, far from absolute, and in the actual religions of the Greek cities it was little more than nominal. In Pindar, and above all in Æschylus, the conception of the unity of the moral order of the world, in theological phrase the unity of the moral government of the world, leads to the exaltation of Zeus to a supremacy of kind rather than merely of degree; in him is the fulness of the godhead—Zeus is God. These pious poets, however, had no thought of combating the religion of the many gods, nor of reforming it; and in fact made no impression upon it. Their verses were quoted in later times by Jews and Christians as utterances of prophets of a monotheism like their own; but such was not their meaning nor effect.

In China the unity of the moral order is personalized in Tien, Heaven, as Supreme Ruler, under whom the hierarchy of nature powers, conceived as spirits, fulfil their several functions; but here again no further progress toward monotheism in the exclusive sense was made.

Philosophy attained the idea of physical unity through reflection on the unity of nature, or of ontological unity by the idea of the necessary unity of Being, and in either case the One may be called God; but while thinkers created a philosophy which was for them a religion or a substitute for religion, their speculations had no effect on the accepted religions except to detach the intellectual classes from them, a point to which we shall have occasion to recur farther on. The essentially monotheistic religions, Judaism, Christianity, and Islam, had a historical origin different from all these tendencies to unification in polytheism.

Advancing civilization does much to civilize religion. The cultus is enriched and æsthetically refined; inhuman rites are made harmless or are symbolized; immoral myths are ignored, or replaced by inoffensive versions, or allegorized away; loftier and purer ideas of the gods and their relations to men are entertained. But civilization, which in the ancient world was an affair of small superior classes, may go too far or too fast in its improvements for the masses, and, sometimes in conjunction with shifting of population, there may be a revival of little gods in whose presence the small man feels more at home and of rude rites such as he is accustomed to, or to similar appropriation from abroad.

The progress of civilization is intimately connected with man's enlarging knowledge of the world and of himself. Experience and inquiry showed that many of the things the forefathers believed were not so, and that their explanations were childish. Religion, on its animistic assumptions, accounted for everything that was and happened in the world by the doings of voluntary agents, whom it imagined according to the need of the case or the vagaries of mythopoetic fancy. When men advanced from the naïve question "Who did it?" to inquiry into the fact and the cause, mythical answers were excluded as such, and in so far as religion lent its authority to mythology, the rejection of the myths involved disbelief in religion. This chapter lies most clearly before us in the history of Greek thought, but parallels to the outcome are found in India and in China.

Philosophy, which long comprehended what we call science, boldly began with the problem of the origin and constitution of the universe, and essayed to solve it without bringing in gods to help; so far as it concerned itself with them at all, gods, as part of the cosmic order, were themselves to be accounted for. The Ionian naturalists and their successors sought a primordial matter, or world stuff, by transformations of which, through the working of its own immanent energy, in conformity with processes of change observable in the nature around us, the world in all its variety, and everything that comes about in it might be causally explained. The insufficiency of the solutions they proposed should not be permitted to obscure the fact that Thales and those who came after him conceived the problem of the universe in a genuinely scientific way.

Most of the early philosophers seem to have gone their way in complete indifference to religion or the consequences of their theories for religion. Xenophanes, however, assailed with trenchant satire not only the immorality of the gods in Homer and Hesiod but all anthropomorphic notions of the gods, while Heraclitus railed at the senseless and scandalous rites of the popular religions. Leucippus and Democritus in their atomic theory developed a mechanical materialism akin to that of the Indian Carvakas, which logically left no more place for soul than for god, and in both cases the inference that the pleasure of the senses is the only good was promptly and boldly drawn.

Anaxagoras shocked the Athenians by teaching that the sun was a white hot mass of rock larger than the Peloponnesus, and the moon a cold rock of smaller dimensions. He was banished and his books burned for his atheistic astrophysics; but the younger generation, imbued with the rationalism of the sophists, rejected the prescriptive authority of religion as well as of morality. The only rule of opinion and conduct was what seemed to the individual reasonable. The agnostic said that no one could know whether there were any gods or not, still less what they were; others asked how men ever came to imagine or invent them. In the field of ethics they wanted to know why the customs of their unenlightened forefathers or their notions of right and wrong should govern the conduct of men of modern education. And what right has the majority to impose on the individual by law or the tyranny of public opinion a rule which seems to him unreasonable and against his interest?

This ebullition of adolescent free-thinking was brief and limited, but the questions it raised in sceptical or negative spirit, together with those which came from the side of nascent science and speculation, became the problems of more serious philosophy. Gods made in the likeness of men, even though magnified to immensity, could meet the demands neither of a scientific theory of the physical universe nor of metaphysical theories of being and becoming; and the *mos maiorum* with the sanction of religion could no longer be the norm of morals.

The philosophers, Plato and Aristotle on the one hand and the Stoics on the other, endeavored to make religion rational and ethics scientific. Theology became the doctrine of a transcendent Deity with the former, of an immanent divine Reason with the latter, and in the one form or the other thenceforth shaped the religious thought and life of the intellectual classes, or, to be more exact, was their real religion so far as they had any, whatever piety they showed toward the ancestral religions. The great mass of the people went on undisturbed by any movements of thought; the religion of their fathers was good enough for them. Its subsequent history is chiefly external, the influx of foreign gods and cults and of barbarous mysteries, and finally of general syncretism—a history of deterioration rather than progress.

In India also thought outgrew the old gods and their worship, but inasmuch as the thinking was chiefly done in the Brahman caste and was from the beginning metaphysical rather than physical, the outcome was different from that among the Greeks. The idea of unity was indeed approached from the cosmological side, most frequently a deity who evolved a universe out of himself; but this was succeeded by an ontological conception the logical issue of which was an idealistic monism. The Upanishads add the great idea of identity. The real self of man, mistakenly imagined to be individual, is identical with the All-Self, and the end of man's being is to realize this identity. This supernatural end leaves all natural ends behind, and with them the gods who minister to man's natural needs. It is, however, superimposed upon natural religion, not set in opposition to it. In the scheme of life with its four stages, the student and the householder learn the Veda, and fulfil the duties and practise the rites of the ancient religion; in the third period the actual observance falls away, and the man occupies himself with reflection on the deeper, mystical meaning of the rites; finally this also is left behind for meditation on the relation of the soul to the universe and the attainment of the sublime goal.

Such was the orthodox way. In contradiction to it were not only the atheistic atomism of the Carvakas, but the numerous sects such as the Budhists, who denied the authority of the Vedas and the Brahman priests. If they did not deny the popular gods also, they paid them no worship and acknowledged no Lord—no supreme God over them. Of this movement, the effect of which on religion in

India outlasted the sects themselves, there will be more to say farther on. Here it is enough to remark that when the tide ebbed, the ancient Brahmanic religion did not regain its pristine supremacy. For all the reverence and the authority accorded to it, the religions we cover with the name Hinduism had the future; religions of ruder origin, which found the way to combine natural and supernatural ends, good things in this life and better things beyond, as the gift of their gods Vishnu and Shiva, while Brahmanism lives on beside them chiefly in the Brahman caste, and for them also beside rather than instead of one of the Hindu religions. Thus in India also the progress of thought transcended the ancient religion, and did not succeed in carrying it on with itself.

In the field of morals the effect is less marked: the fundamental precepts of the religions and sects of India are substantially the same, whatever differences there may be in principles and motives. The form has always remained preceptive; ethics as a science of conduct apart from religious sanctions has no place in the voluminous Indian literature.

These instances illustrate in different ways the reciprocal relations between religion and culture. They show how knowledge and thought may outrun religion, which then, as by an instinct of self-preservation, becomes a retarding or even a reactionary force. The intellectually and morally progressive elements in society may go so fast and so far as to lose touch with the masses, and instead of doing their part to elevate them, leave them to their incorrigible superstitions. Moreover the development of civilization itself is not a continuous forward movement; the retrogradations are as conspicuous in history as the advances, and sooner or later every civilization in the past has become decadent and ceased to be, carrying down with it the religion which was impotent to check the decline and fall.

I have endeavored thus far to indicate what seem to me to be the primary and most potent factors in the origin and growth of religion. It would be a serious mistake, however, to suppose that they were the only factors. However erroneous we may think it to ascribe the origin of religion to the awe inspired in early men by the majestic march of the heavenly bodies, the imposing order of their movements, or to the æsthetic impression of nature in any form, we have no reason to think that our remote forefathers were altogether insensible to impressions to which many children nowadays spontaneously respond. It was not solely because of their utility, nor solely through the fear inspired by thunder and lightning, that the sun and the moon, that cloud and storm and torrential rain, became the great gods of our Aryan ancestors as they are conceived in the Rig Veda. If men sought to placate or propitiate these powers out of a motive of self-preservation, the attendant emotions of the worshippers must have been at least in a measure due to the awe-inspiring impression of their operations in nature. In other words, æsthetic impressions and the emotions they arouse are not in themselves religious, but they become so by reference to the gods who manifest their power in nature. The same thing is true of the impression produced by the softer aspects of nature, by the beauty of its fair frame. The degree in which the majesty and beauty of nature affect the feeling and thought of men differs very widely among different races in accordance with their environment and racial temperament or endowment.

Art has been from very early stages a companion to religion. It is possible that the oldest delineation of animal forms had a utilitarian motive and that what we should call a magical efficacy was attributed to them. But in the higher stages of religion art is taken into its service. Architecture seems everywhere to have had its first great development in the building of temples, houses for the gods, and in tombs for the eternal abode of the great of the earth. In Egypt, where there are no remains of the palaces of kings, temples succeeded one another on the same sites with increasing magnificence from age to age. The temples of Greece are among the greatest achievements of Greek genius, and down to comparatively recent times temples and churches and mosques have been the summit of architectural art. One who to-day, a stranger to the religion which created them and which they express, stands before the long-deserted temples in the solitude of Pæstum and experiences the elevation of spirit which they inspire, can in some faint degree imagine their effect upon the devout worshippers to whom they meant not only art and history but religion.

The first rude idols were succeeded by representations of the gods according to the conception of the religion. In Greece the gods are in form and feature the idealized perfection of humanity. By the side of the works of the Greek sculptors the images of the Hindu gods—a relatively late development in the Indian religion—with their multiple faces, arms, and legs, strike us as grotesque. It is, however, the grotesqueness of symbolic art, the effort to represent the god as more than human, seeing all things and reaching everywhere by his power. Religion gives to art its conceptions and ideals, but art repays its borrowing with interest. It was not a mere phrase when it was said of the Zeus of Phidias at Olympia, that it seemed to add something to the received religion.

Music is another art which has throughout been intimately associated with religion, and some of whose greatest works have been inspired by it, while, on the other hand, no other art has perhaps contributed so much to arouse religious emotion in the worshippers. The drama, as a representation of myth, is also probably everywhere in the beginning a religious art, and in Greece the highest religious ideas find their expression in the tragedies of Æschylus and Sophocles.

CHAPTER VI

AFTER DEATH

In a former chapter it was shown how the belief arose that the soul, the life and self of a man, in the form of a wraith, survives the body which it leaves at death. The oldest notion probably was that it lingered in the neighborhood of its untenanted body and the scenes of its former life. Sometimes it was imagined that it might suffer by the destruction of the body, or might still need the body, which it inhabited as a kind of shell though it no longer animated it. Pains were then taken to preserve the body by natural or artificial means. In Egypt, to make doubly sure that the soul was not left houseless by the destruction of the mummy, portrait statues were installed in the tomb. This belief is, however, not universal, and the disposition of the body differs widely in different regions and times. It may be left on a raised platform out of the reach of wild beasts, buried in the earth with a heap of stones over it for protection, deposited in a natural cave or an excavation in the rock, or it may be consumed by fire. These various modes are frequently associated with different notions about the abodes of the dead, which are probably in most cases secondary.

The existence of the disembodied soul could only be imagined as a ghostly continuation of the earthly life, for which it was accordingly furnished with weapons, utensils, and ornaments, as well as with supplies of food and drink. This custom and, by inference, the beliefs which originate it are of extreme antiquity, going back in Europe at least to the age of the Cromagnon race, and long antedating any certain evidence of religious or magical rites and notions. In settled communities, and even among nomads whose range brings them annually over the same circumscribed area, the provision of food and drink is commonly renewed from time to time, often at stated intervals. With the advance of civilization tombs are built for the great of the earth, to be the "eternal houses" of the living dead, as in Egypt and China or in the field of the Ægean culture, and equipped with furniture, gold and silver and precious stones, costly fabrics, and every article of use and luxury befitting the estate of the occupants.

Wives and servants were entombed with their masters to minister to them in the other life. In some recently opened tombs in Nubia a whole retinue of officials with their families—hundreds in all—had been walled up in a corridor of the tomb where they died of suffocation. The whole court accompanied their lord to his post in the other world, to resume their station and functions there, just as they might have attended him if transferred to another province in this world. In Dahomey, until European rule made an end of it in the last century, a somewhat similar custom existed. At the death of a king hundreds of men and women, chiefly prisoners of war, were killed at his grave to furnish him with wives and servants in the spirit world, and the contingent was annually supplemented. On a smaller scale the same custom is found in many lands. In most civilized countries, however, these bloody ceremonies are superseded by the deposit in the tomb of substitutes—images of wives and slaves. It is a mistake to call such killings "human sacrifice"; it does not appear that they have any religious motive or association. Nor has the related custom of killing men or animals to carry messages to the other world. The slaughter of enemies at the funeral of a chief or warrior, as at the tomb of Patroclus, is of still another kind, an appeasal by vengeance.

The periodical repetition of the deposit of food and drink at the tomb or elsewhere is in origin nothing but a pious provision for the wants of the deceased, prompted by the same motive that leads to similar care for the wants of living kinsmen, and this filial piety is among some peoples the main motive discoverable in the subsequent history of the custom. It is doubtless always accompanied by an apprehension that the spirits, if neglected, may do harm to those who undutifully neglect them, and this motive sometimes appears to be dominant; but this gives no reason for assuming that fear of ghosts is everywhere the sole origin of the tendance of the family dead, who are normally thought of as friendly. It is a dire misfortune for a man to have no descendants to do him this service when he is dead, and often the community unites to provide at regular times for the whole multitude of spirits who have none to care for them individually. Here undoubtedly the apprehension of harm is more prominent than affection for the unknown dead; and the rite assumes the character of riddance by placation. Besides gifts of food, other things may be done to gratify or appease the spirits of the dead, such as funeral games at the tombs of heroes.

All these things are frequently put under one head, and called offerings to the dead, the cult of the dead, the religion of the dead, and it is believed by some that this is the root of all religion. It is important to discriminate between a tendance of the dead which appears to be solely for their sake—however attended by apprehension of what they might do if neglected—and a tendance in which to this is added the interest of the living. This distinction is best illustrated by the difference between what is called the religion of the dead in ancient Egypt and ancestor worship in China.

In no other parts of the world have these things been so immensely developed, and at a superficial glance the phenomena seem to be the same. But in Egypt the offerings are not accompanied by veneration or petitions—the texts on the tables of offering are magical formulas to convey the gifts to the dead in the other world—nor, so far as appears, by the expectation that the dead will do anything for the living in return. In China, on the contrary, the filial descendants venerate their ancestors, acquaint them with their plans and wishes, beseech their favor, and seek their benevolent interest and assistance. They are powers for whom men not only do something, but from whom they look to get something. In other words, ancestor worship in China has the marks of religion, in the ordinary meaning of the word; in Egypt the tendance of the dead has not.

Food and drink are also one of the earliest and most universal kinds of offering made to other than human spirits, from the fetish up to the great gods. But here again it is an overhasty inference that all such offerings originated by extension of offerings to the dead. They are sufficiently explained by the fact that men inevitably imagine all spirits as like themselves, having the same desires and pleased by the same things. The similarity of the customs, however, would naturally tend to a further assimilation of conceptions between disembodied human spirits and spirits recognized in phenomena of nature or other activities in the savage's world, where no difference of kind is recognized between the two. The souls of dead men contribute their full share to the hosts of mischievous demons. A man who was a terror in his lifetime for violence or for witchcraft is all the more terrible when he becomes an invisible malicious spirit whose proximity is evident only when the mischief is done, and who is harder to drive away by aversive magic or to placate by gifts than the living man. On the other hand, the souls of valiant chiefs and of famous Shamans, expert practitioners of beneficent magic, become champions and defenders of their fellows.

The clan gods, who play an important part in certain stages of religion, were often in fact clan heroes of nearer or remoter times, or were believed to have been such. Imagination pictures them in the same character and activities in which they lived among men, and that not in the ghost world but in this, leading their clansmen in the fight or the foray, sometimes even seen by friends or foes at the head of the host, or giving wise counsels through the oracle. Even in more advanced religions great war-gods may be eminent generals of former times, and inventors of the arts of civilization are deified, or the gods of those arts are identified with legendary inventors, as in China. Not only do human spirits thus become gods, but conversely, gods of other origin may come to be believed to have once been men, as is generally thought to be the case with some of the Greek heroes, by a kind of *deminutio capitis*.

Frequently the souls are imagined to go to some gathering place of all the dead (at least of their own people), remote from the haunts of men, in some distant region of the earth, on the other side of a sea, or beyond a river that the living cannot cross, or to ascend to the sky by the path of the milky way, or in the bark of the sun-god. Others put this abode of the shades underground, a dismal cavern in the heart of the earth like the Babylonian Aralu, the Hebrew Sheol, the Greek Hades, or, with another imagery, the Egyptian realm of Osiris, the dead god. When various notions concurred, as in Egypt, they were easily harmonized by the belief, common among savages, that man has more than one soul, a ghost soul, or wraith, that inhabits the tomb or the nether world, and a spirit soul that flies away to a spirit world, and is therefore often imagined as winged, in Egyptian art a bird with a human head, in Greek a butterfly, Psyche.

Social distinctions establish themselves among the dead earlier than moral. The great of this earth get a place of their own apart from the vulgar herd, as they have in burial, some Elysian Plain at the ends of the earth such as Homer describes, or Islands of the Blessed, or the Fields of Earu, where the Egyptian nobles employed their everlasting leisure in playing checkers, while porcelain slaves, made real by the magical word, did their work for them on the canals and in fields of giant wheat. As in these cases, the land of the favored dead is often the abode of the gods, to whose company kings and heroes are admitted as at least half divine.

In Egypt we see with peculiar clearness how a place after death in the boat of the sun, which was originally the exclusive prerogative of the king as the son of Ra, the sun-god, was extended to such as had no pretension to so august a lineage; and how the deliverance from the perils of the nether world in the religion of Osiris was in time appropriated by all classes. The masses, by providing themselves with guide books to Hades, magical formulas and passwords, and protective amulets, usurped the privileges of their betters in another world, if they had no aspirations to democratic equality in this.

The beginnings of what we may call a heaven—though not always or even commonly in the heavens—are here obvious. The opposite, the first threatenings of hell, are found in the consigning to a place apart of men who were guilty of monstrous crimes—a kind of *post-mortem* outlawry. In the Rig Veda the poet invokes Indra and Soma to hurl such "into prison, into fathomless darkness, whence none shall emerge." They have "prepared for themselves that deep place." Into the picture of Hades in the Eleventh Book of the *Odyssey*, the dismal abode of all the shades, were introduced by a later hand the figures of Tityos, Tantalos, Sisyphos, undergoing their several ingenious torments for offenses against the gods. It is to be noted, however, that none of these are mere men, and that their offenses are personal to the gods and in only one case also moral.

The abode of the gods and of the great of earth becomes in time the reward of the conspicuously good of less eminent station. The standard of fitness for this distinction is primarily religious, rather than moral. The good man is he who is most scrupulous in religious observances, most abundant in sacrifices and homage to the gods, most liberal to their ministers. In the Brahmanic religion such men go to the heaven of the gods, whither their good works have preceded them, and enjoy the reward of their piety in celestial bliss. The opposite fate awaits not only the flagrantly wicked, as in the olden time, but those who neglect religion and store up no such merit above. So the priests classify the good and the bad.

The moralizing of the hereafter is a later stage. It is represented in Egypt by the Osirian judgment portrayed in the 125th chapter of the *Book of the Dead*, according to the current numeration. Here the dead man is conducted to the judgment hall, and there makes his solemn protestation of innocence of a long catalogue of misdeeds against gods and men—chiefly the latter. The moral standard is that of an advanced civilization, and in parts of notable elevation. The conscientiousness of the profession is tested by weighing the man's heart in balances against an ostrich feather, the attribute of the goddess Truth, while Thoth, as clerk of the court, records the verdict. The justified man is led into the sanctuary where Osiris is seated on his throne, while the fate of the condemned is grimly hinted by the figure of a monster called the "Devouress" who squats open-mouthed beside the scales. From a frieze a long array of assessors of the court look down on the scene.

The moral condition of man's destiny in the hereafter in this chapter of the *Book of the Dead* did not supersede the very different representations in other parts of that heterogenous collection, in which good and bad alike are exposed to the perils of the nether world and come safely through them only by knowing what to expect, and the charms proper to be used in each emergency. The Egyptians had in fact so long been used to assure their safety beneath the earth by magical means that they employed charms and amulets to protect themselves against a merited condemnation in the Osirian judgment, including an adjuration to a man's own heart (conscience) not to contradict his profession of innocence.

The case is peculiarly instructive. The whole history of religions shows that if a high moral standard is set up and man's destiny is to be determined solely by his guilt or innocence, self-knowledge will drive him either to seek a religious remedy, or, in the lack of that, to fall back on a magical one, or, as is often the case, to make assurance doubly sure by combining the two. How much influence the Osirian judgment had in the subsequent history of religion in Egypt is unknown; that it did not transform it is certain.

From the separation of the conspicuously good and the flagrantly bad at death, religion went on to universalize the division—*all* the good and *all* the bad, however the two classes were constituted—and depicted the blessedness of the one and the misery of the other. The former went to the realm of the gods, wherever that was, and lived immortally in the company of gods and heroes and the good and great of all generations, while the bad suffered not only the privation of this good, but endured the worst evils men could think of. In some cases the two classes go to their own places as of themselves, or they are sorted out by an automatic device, such as a log thrown across a chasm, which the good cross safely while the bad fall off, as was imagined by some of the American Indians, or the Cinvat bridge which serves the same end in Zoroastrianism. Other religions conceive the diverse fate of men as the sentence of inexorable judges, before whom the disembodied souls are forthwith conducted to be tried.

The oldest idea of retribution is retaliation—an eye for an eye, a tooth for a tooth—and when imagination employed itself in picturing this retaliatory justice, it fitted the torment to the offense, and in the end, as in India, divided hell into a multitude of compartments, each with appropriate tortures for particular kinds of sinners.

Among many savages it is believed that the souls

of the dead come back into other bodies, quickening the embryo in the mother's womb or taking up its abode in the infant body at birth. It is also a common notion that human souls may enter into the bodies of other animals. Such metamorphoses may be wrought by the malice of sorcerers or by the vengeance of demons or gods; a man may himself assume such a form by magic. But the re-embodiment of souls after death and their fortunes or misfortunes in the subsequent life may also be believed to be determined by their character in a former life. A violent and ruthless man, who had the disposition and behavior of a tiger, may come back as a real tiger, more cunning and cruel than a mere tiger with a proper tiger's soul, and be hunted to death with an energy and persistence fitting his extraordinary dangerousness.

In India these primitive notions were taken up, as early at least as the Upanishads, into higher religious thought, and generalized. Character makes character: "the doer of good becomes good; the doer of evil becomes evil." Below this high philosophical level, the doctrine prevailed that every soul was re-embodied as man or beast in a form and state, and with a consequent lot in life, determined by its character in its former existence. And eventually not by character as a totality or an average. Every single act had its consequence; it was like a seed which in due time bore its fruit according to its kind, or, to express it in our way, it was a cause which produced its proper effect by inflexible natural law. This is the doctrine of *Karma*, "the deed," which thenceforth dominated all Indian thinking about man's destiny. What added to the terror of the doctrine is that the round of death and birth had neither beginning nor end; from eternity to eternity an infinite series of re-embodiments under the law of Karma runs on, each life a link in an endless chain.

The law of Karma is not an ordinance of the gods. So far from creating or administering it, the gods themselves are subject to it; they also are bound on the endlessly revolving wheel of rebirth. There is no judge and no judgment; no punishment, no repentance or amends, no remission of sins by divine clemency. It is just the inexorable causal nexus of the eternal universe itself. So firmly rooted was this conviction that it could go on in original Buddhism without any soul to transmigrate, Karma alone connecting one life with another.

The belief in retribution for the deeds of this life in the heaven of the gods or in an appropriate hell was long established in India before the consistent development of the doctrine of Karma, and the two were harmonized by interposing the finite rewards of heaven and the finite punishments of hell between every two earthly lives, precisely as we find it subsequently in Plato.

In Greece new notions about the fate of man after death gained wide currency in the sixth century, and had thenceforth large influence both in religion and philosophy. The starting-point here was the belief, perhaps derived from the Thracians by way of the Bacchic-Orphic religions, that a happy immortality belongs by nature only to divine beings; it is indeed their supreme prerogative. Human nature is mortal, and the blessed lot of the immortals in their Elysium, bright with eternal sunshine, with its fragrant airs and sweet sounds, stands in the strongest contrast to the cold darkness of the miry pit which is the final abode of the undivine. The older Hades was also dismal gloom, but new horrors were added to it by barbarian imagination. This hell is not the punishment of sin, but the fate of man because he is man and not god.

It has already been remarked that the notion of re-embodiment which we call the transmigration of souls is found in many parts of the world among races on low planes of culture. The question where man's soul comes from is in fact as natural, though perhaps not as early, as the question whither it goes.

A belief in transmigration is attributed to the Thracian Getæ, and it is not improbable that it came into Greece from the same quarter and by the same channels as the notions described in the preceding paragraph. In literature it first appears upon the scene in Sicily and Southern Italy, and achieved a place in Greek philosophy through Pythagoras and Plato. A reminiscence of its Thracian origin may be confusedly preserved in the legend which brings Zalmoxis into connection with Pythagoras. The Greeks thought that it came from Egypt; many modern scholars believe that the idea was imported from India.

The Greek doctrine is, however, significantly different from the Indian as it has been outlined above. For the Greeks the soul is a fallen divinity, which is here in this sublunary world and imprisoned in a material mortal body in consequence of sin. Pindar speaks vaguely of "the ancient guilt"; Empedocles of bloodshed and perjury. By a decree of the gods, one of the divine beings (*daimones*) who has committed such offenses is condemned to wander thrice ten thousand seasons (10,000 years) far from the blessed, being born through all that time in all manner of forms of mortal creatures, exchanging one grievous path of life for another. In these earthly lives the soul is subject to physical and moral defilement; the body is the tomb of the soul, or its prison-house, its transient tabernacle, its vesture of flesh, its filthy garment. In Greece, as in India, the belief in metempsychosis was combined with the earlier notions of retribution in another sphere of existence; a thousand years of Hades are interposed between successive embodiments on earth. The souls which thus expiated their original fault, and, mindful of their higher nature, kept themselves pure from the temptations of sense and the pollution of things unclean, were at length released, and regained their primal state.

As in ancient religions generally, guilt is conceived as defilement; the remedy in the Pythagorean scheme is physical purification by an ascetic regimen and intellectual catharsis by the philosophic life. Substantially the same ideas appear in Plato, with the important difference that the origin of the evil is not a mythical crime: the fall of the soul is within the soul itself, the failure of the intellectual element to master the passions and appetites; and inasmuch as this disaster is intellectual and moral, the remedy is not found in physical or magical remedies, but in the clarification of the intellect by philosophy and the mind's recovery of its mastery in the soul by virtue.

Where men came to entertain such more definite

notions about a future existence, whether they imagined hells of torment for the misdeeds of this life, or an endless round of rebirths determined by character in antecedent existences, whether they thought of the soul as a fallen divinity condemned to expiate "the ancient guilt," or lapsed from its high estate by the subjection of reason to lower impulses, or of the miry pit in which all the dead wallow because they are not divine, men's minds were more and more preoccupied with what is after death and all its possibilities of woe, and therewith religion entered on a new stage. Hitherto men had sought through religion only security against natural ills and perils such as they had experience of in this life, and a sufficiency of the good things that nature could give for their enjoyment. So far as they concerned themselves about the after-life, it was to insure a continuation of the same enjoyment there by provision of things needful for it. Now the primal motive of self-preservation made them turn to religion for a way of escape from the terrible evils with which imagination, once stimulated to the task, filled the hereafter, and for the assurance of a blessed immortality like that of the gods.

It has already been remarked more than once that the character of a religion is primarily determined by what men seek in it, and this new demand for a good that lies beyond the mortal life and surpasses all finite goods created a new type of religion, with corresponding changes in the ideas of the powers to which man turns for salvation and of the things he must do to secure it.

The religions we have previously considered may be called natural religions, in the sense that what men seek in them are natural goods, the good things of this life. Those to which we now turn our attention might correspondingly be named supernatural religions inasmuch as they answer man's desire for the good things of another life, goods beyond the nature we know. "Supernatural" has, however, so long been used to designate not the end but the divine origin of certain religions that it is inexpedient to use it in an entirely different sense. They have frequently been called "redemptive religions," an attempt, apparently, to English the German term, *Erlösungsreligionen*. In the meaning naturally put on the word "redemptive," Christianity is the only one of them properly so called. Since their characteristic is that they present themselves as ways of salvation, a more suitable name would be "soteric religions." The name is, however, of less consequence than the recognition of the fact that they are a new kind and constitute a class by themselves. Between them and the older natural religions there was no necessary conflict, for the old religions had to do only with the public and private interests of this world, while the new concerned themselves solely with the fate of the individual beyond the tomb, and since the former are real and permanent interests, men pursued them in the accustomed way. The old religions were, moreover, the religions of political communities, or states, into which a man is born, and by this fact is bound to worship the gods of his people or country with the established ceremonies, whatever else he may be moved to do to save his own soul. Sometimes the law may prohibit the introduction of new gods and strange rites; but the pains and penalties of human law have always in the end proved ineffective to deter men from resorting to them for deliverance from the worse evils of the other world.

It is improbable that in general the posthumous perils of the soul profoundly affected the unimaginative multitudes, for whom present ills were a sufficiently absorbing preoccupation. But it is evident that for many, salvation after death—to condense it into our familiar phrase—became a matter of grave concern, and led them to addict themselves to the religions or philosophies which professed to have the secret of it. In some periods and in certain classes the good and evil that lie beyond death have acquired such a preponderance in men's thought that mundane goods even in the richest measure seem to be worthless by comparison, and the enjoyment of them or desire for them, by engrossing man's interest and making him heedless of what comes after, are regarded as the great hindrance to salvation, so that the renunciation of the world and all earthly goods becomes its first negative condition, and an ascetic regimen, physical as well as moral and intellectual, its positive method. This has had its fullest development in the philosophies or philosophized religions for which salvation is essentially the emancipation of the soul, conceived as pure intellect, from the bondage of matter and sense, and the realization of its divine nature.

The soteric religions differ very widely among themselves in consequence of their different antecedents, peculiarities of race temperament, culture, history, and other circumstances. The influence of individual prophets, founders, reformers, thinkers, is also much more strongly impressed on them than on the natural religions. The way of salvation is primarily determined by the nature of the evil to be escaped and the good to be achieved, and of their causes.

The way of salvation must take a totally different direction where the happiness or misery of man after death is conceived as divine retribution, the misdeeds of men against the gods or their fellows being punished by imprisonment and torment in hell while the goodness of the good is rewarded by blessed immortality in the abode of the gods, and where God cannot only punish but forgive, from what it has when every single act, word, and even thought of man produces a corresponding fruit in another existence by an inflexible law of cause and effect from which the very gods are not exempted, as in religions of India. Still different must the way of salvation be where immortality is an attribute of divinity, of which human nature as such is incapable.

Finally, religions of this type have affected one another in various ways, and been affected by the natural religions which surround them. A morphological classification on any principle is peculiarly difficult, and no consistent scheme is wholly satisfactory. It will serve our purpose best to make one class of the religions which not only present themselves as a way of salvation after death for individuals, but set as an ultimate goal the triumph of good over evil in the realm of nature as well as in the world of men and spirits, and the transformation of this earth into a fitting abode for the good in a transfigured bodily existence; while in the second class we include the various religions in which the

AFTER DEATH

idea of salvation is the deliverance of the individual soul from embodied existence in a world of matter and sense. The former are emphatically theistic religions, and their gods are rulers of this world and givers of good in it as well as saviors in another. The latter may be monistic or pantheistic, theistic or atheistic. The former are also essentially ethical, assigning to man a part, with God, in bringing about the good world that is to be. To the first category belong Zoroastrianism, Judaism in its orthodox form, and Mohammedanism; to the second the soteric religions and philosophies of India and of Greece, and the native and foreign mysteries of the Hellenistic-Roman world. Christianity, as we shall see, is a fusion of the two.

CHAPTER VII

WAYS OF SALVATION

OF the religions which look forward to the complete triumph of good over evil on this earth, the oldest is that which, after the name of its founder, we call Zoroastrianism, or by the name of its God, Mazdaism. The beginnings of this religion are involved in impenetrable obscurity. So much is clear, that it was not the natural evolution of an Iranian nature religion, but a prophetic reform or revolution within such a religion. As the wave of reform lost force in its extension, and other branches of the Iranian race, or peoples of other races brought under its empire, adopted the religion, much of the older Iranian religion and many foreign elements were absorbed in Zoroastrianism; but it never lost its distinctive character.

The old Iranian religion was a natural polytheism closely related to that of their Aryan kinsmen in India. The same gods belong to both races, their mythology has large common elements, the peculiar features of the cultus are the same. Zoroaster rejected all these gods with their priesthood, and abolished the bloody sacrifices. There is only one god, whose significant name is Mazda, Wisdom, with the title Lord (Ahura Mazda); most intimately associated with him are Good Mind (Vohu Mano), his first creation (good intelligence, purpose, disposition), and Asha (Right, as conformity to the moral order), Sovereignty, Piety, and other immortal beneficent powers. Of the ancient cultus Zoroaster preserved only the care of the sacred fire and the libation of Haoma, corresponding to the Indian Soma offering. On the other hand, he put a greatly heightened emphasis on the ethical side, condemning much in the hereditary customs of his people, and prescribing others in accordance with the new religious principles.

The reform was involved from the outset in conflict with the old religion and all its supporters, priests, rulers, and people. The reformer's world was divided into two camps, those who were for the reform and those who were against it, the followers of truth and the partisans of the lie, and the same division was run through everything. Over against the one wise and good God were the gods of the old religion, who, in their opposition to the true God, became the demons of the new; over against the Iranian believers were their Turanian foes; over against an agricultural and pastoral civilization, the predatory hordes on the borders; over against domestic cattle, wild beasts and venomous reptiles; over against the grass and grain that gave food to man and beast, all harmful and poisonous plants; and so on through every sphere of the natural and supernatural.

Those who joined the reform did so of their own choice, and so did those who refused it. The generalization of this experience led to the conviction that every man, of his own free will, enlists in the army of truth and righteousness and goodness or in that of the enemies of all these. The world is thus a great battle-field, in which not only all intelligent beings but all things else, even climates, are arrayed on one side or the other. This conflict goes back to the beginning of the present age of the world; it has its prototypes in the two primal spirits, the good, or beneficent spirit, and the evil, or baleful spirit, which at the beginning chose good and evil respectively. It is the age-long war between Ahura Mazda and Ahriman—God and the Devil, we should say. It will end in the complete triumph of the Lord, and the discomfiture of all that opposes him. Then good will prevail universally, and all evil be everlastingly destroyed. The world will be transformed into an abode of the blest; hell itself, purified by fire, will be annexed to the habitable earth to enlarge its borders.

WAYS OF SALVATION

The earliest teaching of the religion was that this crisis in the history of the world was close at hand, and that therefore it behooved every man to enlist without delay on the side whose victory was near and sure, before the day of the fiery ordeal came and it was too late. On that day not only the living would appear in the great assize, but the bodies of the dead would be recreated and reunited with their former souls to receive their reward or suffer their doom according to the side on which they had striven in life. The good should be immortal in a transfigured bodily existence on a purified and transformed earth from which every evil thing was forever banished; while the bad suffered the torment of fire.

As time went by, and the great crisis of history did not arrive, the fortune of souls between death and this postponed judgment was determined on the same principle. Three days after death the souls were conducted before the judges of the dead, who weighed their good and evil deeds—among which their religion weighed heavily—in balances that never swerved a hair from even justice. Thence they passed to the ordeal of the bridge stretched over a fathomless gorge. For the good it was a broad highway, and on the other side they passed through successive vestibules of good thoughts, good words, good deeds, into the light which surrounds the Lord himself; for the bad it was narrow as the edge of a sword, and they hurtled into the abyss below, there to abide till the day of resurrection and the last judgment.

There was but one way of salvation: the acceptance of the sole true religion and conformity to its sacred law. This law, at least as we know it in the later development of the religion, was in large part concerned with the avoidance of all things and acts that defiled with a demonic contagion, and with rites of purification or expiation—a disinfection from such contagion. Extravagant penances are imposed on transgressors, and a confession of sins belongs to the office for the dying. But the primary content of the law was moral: good thoughts, good words, good deeds, is the ever-recurring formula; and good is all that which conduces to the victory over evil in physical nature as well as in the life of society, and to the triumph of the true religion. It is an essentially ethical religion.

Zoroastrianism is an eminently militant faith. Man wins his own salvation by strenuous effort for the triumph of the will of a good God realized in a good world—we might say man saves himself by striving with God for the salvation of the world. Flight from the world would be desertion in the face of the enemy; man's calling is to overcome the evil in the world, not to despair of it. There is a deep realization of the evil of the present world, but of the ultimate triumph of truth and righteousness and goodness not a shadow of doubt.

Zoroastrianism was from the beginning much concerned with what is after death. The prophet made it a chief motive for the conversion of individuals to his reform. It was quite otherwise with the national religion of Israel. There the belief in a divine retribution first established itself in collective form. The apostasy of the nation from the religion of its fathers into the worship of foreign gods provoked the wrath of their own God, which visited itself upon them in national disaster. The prophets, from the eighth century on, laid no less emphasis upon the wrongs that men did to their fellows—the perversion of justice by those in power, the oppression of the poor by the rich in the new economic conditions of the time, and the vices that were associated with the nature religions of the Canaanites or the neighboring nations. God was not only the vindicator of his own honor but the avenger of social wrongs and personal badness. The nation that did such things or tolerated them he would destroy. The agencies of his judgment were the great empires that were beginning to loom upon the horizon of the petty states of Western Syria, first the Assyrians, then the Babylonians. The event ultimately justified the prediction and gave the verification of history to the moral conception of the character of Jehovah.

After the destruction of Jewish nationality by the Babylonians at the end of the sixth century, the older vague notion of individual divine retribution in this life, according to which the good prospered and the bad suffered evils in this life or were cut off in the midst of it, was further developed by an individual interpretation of the prophetic doctrine of national retribution. God became a God of distributive justice who requited every man according to his deserts in kind and measure. The lengths to which orthodoxy pushed its logic in this direction is best seen in the arguments of Job's uncomfortable comforters—a great sufferer must be a great sinner; to deny that is to impugn the justice of God which is a corner-stone of religion. Human experience corresponds very ill to this dogma. The author of the Book of Job strives to refute it, though he finds no theodicy to substitute for it. All he can say is that God's dealings with men are as inscrutable as his operations in nature. A more sceptical attitude to the morality of Providence is seen in the Book of

Ecclesiastes, whose author can discover no difference between the lot of the good and the bad in this world, and no difference in their fate in or after death. For good and bad, for man and beast alike, death is the end.

A welcome escape from the dilemma, which seemed to leave no choice but either to blink the patent facts of experience or to deny the justice of God, was offered by the idea of a sphere of retribution beyond this life. The author of Job apparently knew no such conception; the author of Ecclesiastes rejects it; Jesus, the son of Sirach, ignores it. But in the latter centuries before the Christian era the Jews were in contact with two peoples who had developed doctrines of *post-mortem* retribution. On the one side were the Persians, whose Zoroastrian doctrine was the individual judgment of souls immediately after death; the separate lot of good and bad in happiness or woe until the end of the age; the resurrection of the dead for a universal judgment; the renewal of the earth; and the blessedness of the age to come for the good, while the bad suffered torments. On the other side the Jews became acquainted with the prevailing Greek notions of the native immortality of the soul and of retribution after death in a disembodied state.

To a religion in which the ideas of the justice of

God and his righteous retribution, now individualized, were so strongly established, the extension of the sphere of retribution beyond the tomb, whenever and however the idea may first have come, must have seemed the necessary complement of the doctrine of retribution in this life, and to be essentially Jewish, in whose hands soever they found it. Among the Greek-speaking Jews Hellenistic ideas of immortality were peculiarly attractive, especially to the educated classes, while the progressive part of Palestinian and Oriental Judaism adopted the idea of the resurrection of the body, a final judgment, and a new world for the righteous beyond judgment. In both, the conditions of escape from evils beyond the tomb and participation in future blessedness were adhesion to the true religion with its ethical monotheism, and scrupulous observance of its religious law, written and unwritten, in its ceremonial as well as its moral part. For it was all one divine revelation of the true religion—what men were to believe about God and what duties God required of men.

The Jews were well aware that upon such conditions, if they were construed strictly, no man could be saved; for no man does, or can, fulfil the whole law. God, too, knew this before he ever gave the law, before he ever created frail man. Accordingly, in his mercy he provided repentance as a remedy for sin. Here again the prophetic doctrine of national repentance was individualized, and all the promises in the prophets of the restoration of God's favor to the penitent nation were appropriated for the individual. Repentance is the cardinal doctrine of salvation in Judaism.

The Hebrew word for repentance means literally turning about or turning back; its proper equivalent in English is "conversion." It is the turning away from evil courses of whatever nature to good, to God, and to willing obedience to his will. The sincerity of repentance is proved by its result: the genuinely penitent man does not repeat the sin of which he has repented, even under strong temptation and with full opportunity.

All the sacrifices and expiations of the law, including the great expiation of the Day of Atonement, do not expiate sin or secure God's forgiveness and the remission of the penalty without such repentance; repentance is the condition of the efficacy of all rites. Men are warned not to imagine that they can sin, expecting to make it good with God by repentance, and then go and sin again. That is no repentance; it is nothing but a futile attempt to deceive God, who knows the hearts of men. But even the greatest sinner, if he be sincerely repentant, is assured of the forgiveness of God, and that even to the end of his life. What a Christian theologian might call the temporal consequences of sin are not always annulled by repentance, but in death itself the last remainder is expiated, and the blessedness of the soul in the intermediate state and man's participation in the renewed world that lies beyond the final judgment are secure.

In both Zoroastrianism and Judaism, faith in the one true God and in the revelation he has made through his prophets is fundamental; but in neither is this requisite so explicitly formulated as it is in Mohammedanism. The Moslem profession of faith, "There is no god but God (Allah) and Mohammed is the messenger of God," is the corner-stone of the religion and the indispensable condition of salvation. In thus making the acceptance of Mohammed, the prophet or apostle, an article of faith and condition of salvation Islam avows itself the sole true religion, in express opposition to Judaism and Christianity with their prophets, Moses and Jesus, both of whom, indeed, delivered to their times a revelation from the same one God, but revelations which had been corrupted by those to whom they were committed, and were antiquated by the new and final revelation through Mohammed.

Mohammed's ideas of the unity of God and of God's insistence on the recognition of his unity were derived from Judaism. From it came also the expectation of an imminent crisis and God's judgment upon all polytheists and idolaters. From the same source came the resurrection of the dead, a paradise of delights for believers, and a hell of torment for unbelievers. Mohammed's own idea of Paradise, with its verdant plains, its abundant streams and pools of water, its balmy airs and sweet odors, is the most perfect landscape a dweller in the arid and burning valley of Mecca could imagine; the imagery of the fiery hell is less original. The books of account in which every man's good and evil deeds are set down to be produced at the judgment day, and of the judgment bridge, were probably borrowed by him from the Arabian Jews, but are ultimately of Zoroastrian origin, as we have seen. What is characteristic is the emphasis upon faith as the *sine qua non* of salvation, with its converse, that no true believer shall finally be left in hell, whose fires are for such purgatorial, while all heathen and misbelievers burn there everlastingly.

While Judaism was a national religion which in later ages became a religion of the other world also, and consequently opened its way of salvation to all who were naturalized in the Jewish people by circumcision and baptism, Mohammedanism was in its beginnings a way of salvation for individuals, which became the national religion of the Arabs by the conversion to it of the whole population of the peninsula, and in the next stage the state religion of the Arab empire.

All these religions were fundamentally monotheistic in principle, though their success brought into them much popular polytheism and demonology, more or less disguised. In them all God had given a law covering the whole of human life, belief, worship, and observance. Transgression or neglect was punished by him in this world, and faith and obedience were rewarded. At death the souls of the good and the bad were separated, and abode in blessedness or misery until the last day. When that day came the bodies of the dead would be recreated by God and reunited with their souls, to stand at the bar of God in the last judgment. The scene of the eternal beatitude of the saved was originally this earth, renewed and glorified, but the imagery is often unearthly—the celestial Garden of Eden displaces the terrestrial. In none of them is the good world that is to be the outcome of an historical process; it is ushered in by the intervention of God in a great catastrophe. But in all of them good men toil and strive for the supremacy of the true religion, the triumph of truth and right, in the way of God's appointment. Faith in God and conformity to his revealed will is the way of salvation. Sin is violation of God's law, and the greatest sin is unbelief, the rejection of God himself.

Each of them, like Christianity, presented itself as the sole completely true religion and exclusive way of salvation, and as such destined in the end to be the universal religion of mankind. For the achievement of this destiny its adherents were to strive by every means in their power, a conviction which gave a distinctive motive and character to their propaganda.

Of a wholly different type from the religions we have hitherto been considering, are those which originate in the belief that immortality belongs only to divine natures, while man by the very constitution of human nature is mortal, subject to the miseries of this life, to death, and after death to a miserable existence beneath the earth—a survival which is the conscious privation of life. As was said in the preceding chapter this conception seems to have been at home among Thracian tribes, whence it made its way into Greece with the religion of Dionysus and his rivals or satellites by the sixth century B. C. With it came crude notions of the way by which man might escape his natural fate and secure a blessed immortality. If none but gods can be immortal, man can attain immortality only by becoming god, and can be assured of the result only by the experience of being god. The myths of Dionysus, Zagreus, Sabazios, Orpheus, were of a peculiarly savage character; they told of a wild god with his train of followers rushing madly through forests and over mountains, of a god who was torn to pieces by his enemies and brought to life again. The saving experience of godhead was therefore sought by going through what he did, re-enacting as it were his tragedy. In these orgies his devotees worked themselves up to a pitch of possession—enthusiasm is the Greek word—in which they were invaded by the god, and, their own consciousness being suppressed, they revelled in the god-consciousness. Similar phenomena of collective possession are not unfamiliar in savage religions and are cultivated for various ends, but in the religions we are now considering they became a way of salvation from the evils that are beyond the tomb.

In the rites of Dionysus or of Orpheus one of the means by which the end was attained was the rending asunder of the living body of an animal sacred to the god—in more primitive conception the divine animal—drinking its warm blood and devouring the palpitating flesh in which was the life of the god, thus becoming physically partakers of the divine nature, as the savage warrior by eating the heart or the liver of his fallen enemy appropriates to himself the courage and strength of his foeman. In Greece such orgiastic and cannibal rites were attenuated by civilization; but the enthusiasm in which man has the experience for the time of being god, of living and suffering as god, continued to be the earnest of his immortality.

To such participation in the godhead it was necessary that the native corruption of human nature should be purged away, and the initiatory rites took the form of purification by bathing in water, by smearing the candidate with mud and rubbing it off, or by the use of blood for the same purpose.

Of native Greek origin were the mysteries of Eleusis in Attica. The ancient myth, as we read it in the Homeric Hymn to Demeter, told of the maiden Korè who was carried off to the nether world by its sovereign, Pluto, of the inconsolable grief of her mother, Demeter, and how she kept the seed corn in the fields from germinating till the celestial gods in pity intervened and arranged that Korè should spend the winter season of each year below, returning to the earth when the spring flowers blossomed. This is plainly one of a large class of vegetation myths in which the wintry death of nature and its springtime revival, or in other climates its death in the burning summer and resurrection in season of rains, is told as a story of what happened once upon a time to persons, divine or human. So far as can be inferred from cryptic allusions, in the celebration in the great hall at Eleusis scenes from the myth were exhibited to the *mystæ*, perhaps in *tableaux vivants*, and—what was very likely the original core of the mystery—objects that were once the apparatus of magical rites to make the crops grow, now become symbols of the mystery faith. The secrets of the performance were well kept, but there was no secret about their significance. Those who had seen these things carried away an assured hope of a blessed immortality. There was no esoteric doctrine; the initiates, as Aristotle says, were put in a certain frame of mind—we should say, they had a certain religious experience—which gave them the conviction that, like the grain of wheat cast into the earth, though they died they should live again.

The Eleusinian mysteries were more decorous than the popular Dionysiac-Orphic orgies. Many of the foremost men in the Greek and Roman world were numbered among their initiates, and they continued to attract such even down to the end of the fourth century of the Christian era.

In the Hellenistic and Roman age other religions centring around the myth of the god who had died a violent death and been brought to life again offered a similar salvation to those who in their way identified themselves with the god in his death and resurrection. The most important of these were the mysteries of Attis, the beloved of the great mother goddess of Phrygia; the Egyptian mysteries of Isis and Osiris, or Serapis; and the Syrian mysteries of Adonis, whose myth resembles that of Attis. Farther back in this line are the Babylonian Ishtar and Tammuz; but there, so far as we can see, the desired end was magical deliverance from physical death, not divine immortality. The doctrine of the Mithras mysteries can only be guessed at; it was apparently of a different kind. The salvation it offered was, however, one of the most popular of the time.

In contrast to the religions of this life, which were the public affair of the city or state, and of the individual as a member of the political-religious community into which he was born, the religions of the other life were personal concerns, in which each man sought salvation for himself in the way in which he believed it was to be found. The mysteries—

churches or conventicles we should call them, if we spoke our own language—were voluntary associations of initiates, which sought to make converts to their several gospels, inviting men to seek their salvation in them, while they jealously concealed from the uninitiated what was done in their secret assemblies.

The characteristic of this class of religions is that the assurance of a blessed immortality is found in becoming divine through union or identification with a divinity, generally one who on earth had died a violent death and been restored to a deathless life. The union is attained sometimes in enthusiasm, sometimes by sacraments, in which man becomes, physically or symbolically, a partaker of the divine nature. In most religions of the type both methods were employed. Initiation into the mystery and participation in its rites and experiences was the indispensable condition of salvation, originally its sole condition. The higher moral sense of the Greeks took offense at the ignoring of character: it was absurd to think that a notorious highwayman went at death to everlasting bliss because he was initiated, while a model of virtue like Epaminondas was lost because he was not. But ethical reflections of this kind did not succeed in making virtue necessary in the mystery salvations. Men wanted to take their assurance unconditionally.

CHAPTER VIII

SALVATION: RELIGION AND PHILOSOPHY

In India three ways of future blessedness are recognized as orthodox, that is, as consistent with the Veda: The Way of Works, the Way of Knowledge, and the Way of Devotion. The first of these, the Way of Works, is the ancient Vedic doctrine that by good works, the best of which are sacrifices to the gods and liberal gifts to the Brahman priests, man may acquire for himself a permanent abode in the heaven of the gods where his meritorious deeds are laid up in store for him. When the belief in the transmigration of souls, and rebirths determined by the deeds of a former existence, became the nightmare of the Indian mind, the heaven of the gods attained by sacrifice and prayer and generosity to the priests could no longer be a lasting abode. No deeds could liberate man from the law of the deed. The problem which all the religions and philosophies of India had thenceforth to face was not how man may earn a place in the heaven of the gods, but how he may escape from the eternal round of predestined rebirth.

The Way of Knowledge offered such an escape,

and, from the age of the Upanishads down, the goal of philosophy, monist or dualist, was the attainment of the intuitive knowledge which *is* liberation. To this subject we shall return in a subsequent connection.

Under the influence of the new problem, asceticism took on a different significance and a heightened value. Bodily privations, self-inflicted hardships and sufferings, appear in very early stages of religion, and are practised for various motives. One of the most persistent of these is the notion that endurance of suffering in some way increases power, not only what we should call natural or physical power, but powers beyond the ordinary measure of man, and these notions survive in religions higher in the scale. They were long established and widely practised in India.

When the endless series of bodily existences became the great evil, and final emancipation from bodiliness the goal of the seekers of salvation, asceticism had another end. The repression of the body with all its appetites, passions, and even its imperative needs, and the infliction upon it of every kind of hardship, was not only an expression of contempt for the flesh but a means of reducing this "not-self" to the verge of non-existence; for the consciousness of the ascetic "It is not I; it is not mine." Such maltreatment of the body was taken up also into the regimen of the philosophic life; it was a preparatory condition to the attainment of the saving insight into the nature of reality.

In the midst of all this, a striking phenomenon meets us in the history of religion in India, the rise and rapid spread of religions which not only rejected the Vedas and the Brahman priesthood with their Way of Works, but the Way of Knowledge, the metaphysics of salvation in the Upanishads and the philosophic schools. They worship no gods, and they own no Lord (personal supreme God); they abjure metaphysics, and reject all speculations about the Absolute or eternal individual soul-monads. They undertake to show a man what he must do to achieve his own deliverance from the round of rebirth and its endless misery, to be his own savior without the aid of god or man.

In the age and region in which these religions sprung up individuals were seeking the solution of the problem of salvation for themselves by the severest asceticism, and by arts of abstraction and concentration, the practice of Yoga in its contemporary forms, through which the experience of emancipation might be reached in this life; while various teachers who professed to have found the secret of deliverance drew to them a numerous following and became founders of sects or orders. In these circles it was the universal conviction that neither good works according to the Brahmanic conception of them, nor religious learning—the knowledge of the Vedas—can effect the great deliverance, for they do not touch the root of the evil. The universal law of the deed and its fruit applies to good works as well as to bad, and whether the consequence of the deed is a better or a worse lot in a finite hereafter, man is still bound fast on the ever-revolving wheel of existence; deliverance is achieved only when man knows, "It cometh not again."

Among the sects which offered themselves as a way of salvation in that age the two of permanent importance were the Jains and the Buddhists. The former survive to this day in India, but have never spread beyond it. Buddhism, on the contrary, became the first great international religion, and in one form or another spread over all Eastern Asia. Its founder, generally known by his title, Buddha, "The Enlightened One," was born about 560 and died in 480 B. C. Leaving home and wife and child, he had for seven years sought deliverance, first by the extremest privations, and then under the guidance of highly esteemed Yoga teachers, but did not find it. Finally in an hour of penetrating intuition he discovered the root of the evil and the way of release, and began proclaiming to others the fundamental truths and the method of salvation.

The first of the four great truths is the universality of suffering in this life and in the endless chain of lives of which the present is only one link. Upon that point all the seekers of salvation in his time were agreed. The second truth is the origin of suffering in desire. That man desires what can only lead to suffering comes from ignorance of the concatenation of desire, purpose, deed, and consequence. Here again Buddha was in accord with some, at least, of his predecessors. The third of his great truths is that suffering can only be ended by the extinction of desire of every kind; ultimately of the desire for life—the will to be. The last truth is the salutary regimen by which desire may be completely extinguished, the so-called "eightfold path," which leads through a moral and intellectual self-discipline to an inner concentration in which, sensation, perception, intellection, and consciousness itself being suppressed, man experiences in foretaste the endless peace. As in other contemporary schools and sects, this goal is called Nirvana.

In the history of Buddhism, Nirvana has had many meanings, and we have no occasion here to go into disputed definitions. It will suffice for our purpose to take it in the sense of the blessed state of release which comes when the chain of causation that reaches from one life to another has been broken. Nor need we dwell here upon the peculiar attitude of Buddha toward the Ego, the individual self, or soul, whose existence he denies—it is not a substantial soul which passes from one existence to another, but only the Karma of one that is transmitted to another, as, to use his own figure, one lamp is lighted from another, though neither the lamp nor the oil nor the flame is the same.

For the practice of the method by which desire was to be extinguished and Nirvana attained, Buddha, like other religious teachers of his time, established a mendicant brotherhood. Its rule was a middle way between the extravagant privations practised by many and a life of self-indulgence. The body was neither to be maltreated nor pampered, since both extremes are incompatible with the mental and moral discipline through which the goal was to be reached. It was impossible to practise this discipline while living the life of a householder, with its family and social ties. Only one who severed all such ties and devoted himself wholly to the quest of salvation could hope to attain it. Entrance upon this way was by the profession: "I take refuge in the Buddha; I take refuge in the Dharma; I take refuge in the Sangha"—the Teacher, the Truth, the Order.

In primitive Buddhism, salvation was thus in the strictest sense an achievement of the individual for himself and by himself. Buddha had discovered the way and taught it to men; his disciples repeated his teachings, and counselled and exhorted one another about the practice of them; those who had made most progress were an example to the less advanced; the rule provided for a fortnightly general confession through which the faults of the brethren were discovered and corrected. But beyond that no man could help another; even the Buddha himself could not. Nor was there any god who could further a man in his pursuit of salvation, much less bestow it upon him.

The founder was held in reverent affection as the discoverer and teacher of the saving truth; but if in the early days there can be said to have been any object of devotion at all it was the Truth, the Dharma, rather than the Buddha. And when before long, in some circles, Buddha came to be regarded as a supernatural being who had descended to the world from the Tusita heaven to make known to men the way of salvation, it was as teacher, not as savior, that he was venerated. Nor did the doctrine which early emerged in some circles that the

Buddha on earth was above all the limitations of ordinary mankind, or the docetic theory that his body was only a semblance of humanity assumed in his condescension, make any essential change in this attitude. Buddhism made its founder and many of its saints objects of worship in the sense of veneration, but it did not seek from them by this worship either the good things of this life or the supreme good, deliverance from the evils of the beyond. To make the former objects of desire was in the act to renounce the quest of salvation; salvation itself by its very nature could not be bestowed by god or man. In the expansion of Buddhism, like other religions under similar conditions, it took in with its converts such of the old gods as they set the greatest store by, who were legitimized in the character of guardians and defenders of the faith, and as such received religious worship.

Buddha was averse to all speculation as vain and unprofitable, but his followers could not permanently maintain this attitude in the controversy with philosophically minded opponents or in the questionings of their own minds, and in time evolved in their schools metaphysical doctrines of reality—or unreality—which compete in abstractness of content and subtlety of ratiocination with the Vedantists themselves. Under the influence of these ontological theories, the conception of the nature of Buddha underwent a transformation somewhat resembling what Neoplatonic thinkers accomplished in Christian doctrine.

Moreover, the goal had shifted from the attainment by the individual of the character of Arhat (saint) and entrance into Nirvana, to becoming a Buddha, with all a Buddha's essential knowledge and a Buddha's mission. But through all this, the achievement was solely man's own. It was "salvation by man's own power."

Such a salvation is evidently not for all. The sole hope primitive Buddhism held out to its own lay adherents was that by keeping the simple commandments for laymen and by charity bestowed upon the mendicant brothers a man might be reborn with a predisposition to become a monk and thus enter on the way of salvation, and be born in circumstances that made it possible for him to fulfil this purpose. What was true of Buddhism in this respect was true in one way or another of all the orthodoxies and heresies of the age; to those who were not able by renunciation, by transcendental knowledge, by extinction of desire, to save themselves, they had nothing to offer.

It is easy to see, therefore, what an attraction for the masses of men religions possessed which offered the assurance of salvation on more practicable terms; the religions which it is customary to group together under the vague name Hinduism. As natural religions their history doubtless goes very far back, but when they emerge upon our knowledge they had already taken for their sphere the life that is to come as well as that that now is. Two such religions have outgrown all others, or to speak more exactly, have absorbed all the rest, and between them divide the faith and hope of the millions of India. The supreme god of one of them is Vishnu, of the other Shiva. As natural religions they grew up in different regions of India, and even to-day are unequally distributed over the peninsula. The stamp of their natural origin remains ineffaceable, and in many respects they are widely diverse. Their intrinsic differences are multiplied by the innumerable sects to which each of them has given birth. They are, however, fundamentally alike in character with which we are here concerned: in both of them man seeks salvation and deliverance by devotion to a savior god. This is the third of the ways of salvation which, as we have seen, the native analysis distinguishes, the Bhakti Marga.

Bhakti, the specific difference of these religions, is faith; they are religions of salvation by faith. As in other religions of this type, "faith" comprehends in varying proportions belief, trust, and responsive affection, which may rise to mystical exaltation. The emotional element is especially conspicuous in the religion of Vishnu. This god—the supreme god of the religion—has from age to age, when the need of the times was greatest, become incarnate and appeared on earth as a man; and it is to these Avatars ("descents") of Vishnu, especially to his incarnations, Krishna and Rama, that the faith and love of his followers is chiefly directed. The motive of these incarnations is the compassion of God with men and his desire to save them; and those who put their trust in him and show devotion to him in their lives he delivers from the law of rebirth and takes to be with him in the endless bliss of his heaven.

In Buddhism itself a corresponding evolution took place in what are called the Pure Land (or Happy Land) sects. One of the early Japanese exponents of this doctrine reasoned thus: In ancient times, when men were stronger and better than they are now, they were able to achieve salvation by their own power, walking in the Holy Way; but in these degenerate days few, if any, are capable of attaining it thus. If, therefore, the great mass of mankind are not to be helplessly and hopelessly lost, salvation must be extended to them "by the power of another."

Such a salvation is provided by Amitabha Buddha, who ages ago vowed that he would not himself enter into the bliss of attainment unless every man who in devout faith called upon his name might be saved. Those who, putting their confidence in this vow, thus call upon Amitabha are received by him into the Western Paradise, the realm of endless light, where they progress to perfection in knowledge and character. Here, again, religion, in despair of man's ability to save himself, turns as its only hope to the grace of God—for a god in everything but the word, Amitabha is—through faith. When the Jesuit missionaries first made acquaintance of Japan they recognized in the Shingon, the ritualist high church of Japanese Buddhism, a diabolic travesty of their own liturgy; and discovered that the devil had done them another ill turn by planting the Lutheran heresy of salvation by faith alone in Japan to confront them on their arrival.

From the dawn of philosophy it has addressed itself to problems with which religion was concerned. Speaking generally, we may say that its endeavor was to put a rational theory in the place of mythical explanations of the world, its origin, and its working; a valid physical or metaphysical conception of reality and the ground of being in place of naïve assumptions; a rational and moral idea of God in place of popular notions which were neither; a rational ethics in place of a customary morality. Nowhere is this characteristic of philosophy more conspicuous than in its endeavor to solve the problem of salvation, when it had once been raised. In all ages and climes, philosophic conceptions have either given a distinctive character to the religion of thinking men, or have enabled them to satisfy their religious needs outside the traditional religion of their surrounding. It is proper, therefore, to conclude this survey of soteric religions with a glance at philosophy as a way of salvation.

Philosophy began, in India as well as in Greece, with the problems of the physical universe—cosmological problems to which theology had led the way. The reality of the material universe and of the change which is its unchanging character was assumed. Sooner or later, however, thinking was sure to raise the question, What is the nature of reality? and thus to turn to the problems of ontology, or metaphysics. In India this current of thinking is in full tide in the Upanishads. The doctrine which there prevails is that there is but one reality, to which the name Brahman is given. For this metaphysics Brahman is pure being, simple unity which excludes all duality, even that of subject and object in consciousness. As pure intelligence it is immaterial; as self-sufficient it is perfect bliss. The soul or self of man (*atman*) is not only of the same nature, but is the same identical reality. Individuality is the great error, and the cause of all man's ills; for by it man goes from death to another life and so on, as long as he cherishes the illusion of separate selfhood. Salvation, therefore, is possible only through the overcoming of this illusion, and the recognition of the truth, to put it in personal form, that I—or what mistakes itself for I—is nothing else than the one reality itself, and not another. When the self that dreams itself finite and individual realizes that it is the infinite Self, the one and all, then, "it cometh not again." Formulas for this doctrine are "the non-duality of Brahman," or, in another phrase, "*That* (namely Brahman) art *thou*."

This transcendental knowledge is not a doctrine that can be learned and taken on the authority of a teacher, or reached by way of demonstration, or accepted on the ground of its self-evidence. If it is ever attained, it comes as an intuition which brings its certainty in itself. Moral excellence, ascetic exercises, reflection, contemplation carried to and beyond the limits of consciousness, are only means by which a man may put himself in a state in which this transcendent intuition is possible. Here, again, the attainment is man's own; the impassive Brahman has nothing to do with it.

The question was bound to arise, however, if Brahman is the sole reality, one, immaterial, changeless, what is this manifold changing material world which we perceive by our senses; or, to put the question more properly, whence arises the fatal illusion that there is such a world of objects and phenomena, the illusion that I, who am not I, am aware of a world that is not a world. Where is the seat of this illusion? If there be nothing but Brahman, then the illusion must be lodged in it. Into this apparent self-contradiction, and the way in which Shankara sought to extricate himself from it and to reconcile his idealistic monism with its Absolute of which nothing can be said except "*neti, neti*"—"it is nothing that can be thought of it"— with other parts of the Scriptures in which the reality of the phenomenal universe is assumed, and Brahman is regarded as the ground, source, or author of it, we need not here enter, being concerned with this philosophy as a way of salvation and not as a system of metaphysics. Multitudes in India, from the time of the Upanishads down, have sought and found assurance of deliverance in the experience of identity of self with the Over-Self. Like similar philosophies in the West it is a lofty mysticism of purely intellectual type.

Few men are capable of breathing the rarefied atmosphere of such empyrean heights. Much easier for the ordinary mind is some form of pantheistic conception in which the soul of man is an efflux or a particle of the universal soul, with which it is reunited after death, preserving consciousness, or in which it is absorbed at death, merging consciousness. And in India, as elsewhere, men have found no insuperable difficulty in personifying the All, and converting their pantheism into a species of theism. One great school, which, in opposition to Shankara, claims to be the true interpreter of the Vedanta, makes of Brahman—identified with Vishnu and Narayana—a gracious supreme god, object of man's love and devotion, by whose grace he is saved; approximating thus in a lofty religious philosophy the popular forms of Hinduism of which we have already spoken.

In an atmosphere of metaphysics such as that of intellectual India in the centuries that followed the foundation of Buddhism, some Buddhist schools appropriated in different ways an absolute ontology whose filiation with the Vedanta is unmistakable. Of this absolute "Suchness" (*thathata*) not only Gautama, whom we call the historical Buddha, but innumerable Buddhas in all the infinite æons of time and all the regions of n-dimensional space are in some way manifestations. On the other hand, the Buddha nature is in all men, and the realization of this potentiality is the sublime goal toward which the seeker (*Bodhisattva*) presses through existence after existence until the perfection of character and knowledge is attained. In the various systems of the Mahayana, therefore, the end set before the Buddhist is not cessation—Nirvana in the original sense—the cessation of desire and with it the ending of the bond between the doer and his deed, the deliverance from rebirth; what man now strives for is to realize in himself the infinite intelligence and goodness of the Buddha nature which is potential in all men, and to become in some future existence a Buddha and the savior of all sentient beings.

A rival of the Vedantin monism which for a time seriously contested the field with it was the dualistic system of the Sankhya. For it, there was "nature" (*Prakriti*), matter charged with energy, eternally active, composite, ceaselessly changing, and "selves" (*Purusha*), eternal, individual, immaterial, simple, passive monads; unchanging in themselves and untouched by anything that goes on in "nature." To "nature" belongs the psychical apparatus of thinking, feeling, willing, and all its products. The fatal error of man is that he imagines that his *self* is affected by the changeful activity of nature—that it is his *self* that enjoys or suffers, as if a crystal vase should imagine that the red image of a hibiscus flower thrown upon it was a redness in itself. So long as this illusion lasts, the self is involved in the round of rebirth and all its misery. Deliverance is the recognition of the complete independence of the self, its individual absoluteness.

We have already seen that in Greece as well as in India the doctrine of metempsychosis was taken up in the philosophy of the Pythagorean school and by Plato. In both, the soul, a divine nature, is in the world here below and in a body of gross matter as the consequence of a fall. The soul brings with it into this earthly existence reminiscences of its native state, wherein lies the possibility of rousing it to an aspiration to regain it. The body shares the impurity of matter, and to keep the soul from defilement by this contaminating contact and to clarify the intellect by philosophy is the only way to hasten its release.

The fall of souls and their fortunes in successive embodiments was conceived in the form of myth, and this form is preserved in Plato, with whom, however, myth is the transparent vestment of much more profound ideas. We have already noticed that for him the fall is not an unimaginable crime—bloodshed or perjury—in the celestial realm, as in Empedocles. As appears most clearly in the myth of the charioteer and his pair of winged steeds in the Phædrus, the disaster comes from the driver's failure to control the unruly beast—that is, the failure of the intellect to master the soul's lower impulses.

The great contribution of Plato to philosophy is the idea of immaterial reality, which had its origin in Pythagorean observations on the reality of the properties of numbers and geometrical forms on the one side, and in the Socratic theory of the reality of ethical universals on the other, and was developed in the doctrine of ideas. To this realm belong the intellect of man, as well as the supreme intellect, the θεῖος νοῦς. Both are by nature eternal in past and future; the human soul eternally individual. God is not only pure intelligence but perfect goodness, the very idea of the Good; and to regain his native high estate man must not merely purge his intellect of all the illusions of error, but strive to achieve likeness to God in character. Only thus can he realize his true nature and destiny wherein is man's highest good, his perfect and eternal well-being.

Platonism in this aspect is a way of salvation like the great Indian philosophies. But whereas the latter are fundamentally ontological—comprehending in that word their metaphysical psychology—and salvation is achieved by the intuitive apprehension of the relation of the soul to the changeless Absolute, or to multitudinous and changeful nature (*Prakriti*) —morality, and that of a conventional type, being no more than a condition precedent to that attainment—to the Greek, ethics is an integral part of philosophy; the practice of virtue is an imitation of God and a transfiguration into his image. Realized salvation is perfect likeness to God, who is himself the projection into the infinite of the highest ethical ideals of man.

There is an ascetic note in Plato, as in every idealist philosophy. The soul, rising superior to the deceptions of the senses and the seductions of the appetites, emancipating itself from subjection to the body, must collect itself, and, so far as it can, live by itself. This liberation makes man, even on earth, divine and immortal. The philosopher's flight from the world is the putting on of the likeness of God; and when such a one is finally released from mortal existence, the pure soul ascends to be forever with God.

This doctrine attained its ultimate form in ancient

philosophy in Plotinus. On the one hand he pushed the transcendence of the unity of which Plato himself had said that it is beyond knowledge and beyond being, to its extreme consequence in an Absolute to which even self-consciousness must be denied. On the other hand, he endeavors to overcome the dualism of Plato, who posited an eternal primordial matter, and to derive the material universe, with its manifoldness and perpetual change, from the unchanging One. And in the third place, in accordance with the general trend of philosophical and religious thinking in his time, he went far beyond Plato in conceiving the world of matter and sense as inherently evil not only physically but morally.

Premising so much about the conditions of the problem as it presented itself to Plotinus, we may turn to the religious side of his philosophy.*

The soul is by nature divine, of the same essence with deity; its fall is its desire to be something for itself, through which it forgets its father, God, and its own true nature; rejoicing in the exercise of its free will, it strays so far that it loses the consciousness of its origin, "as children early torn from their parents and brought up for a long time away from them do not know either who they are or who their

* In the following paragraphs I have reproduced in part the summary of the teaching of Plotinus from my *Metempsychosis* (1914).

parents were." The double error of the soul is overvaluing earthly things and disprizing itself. But if it can be brought to see the worthlessness of the things it esteems above itself, and to recognize its origin and worth, it has in itself the power of recovery. For, as Plotinus expresses it, "our soul did not wholly descend into the world of sense, but somewhat of it ever abides in the intelligible world." To that world it may mount up again, and dispelling the illusion of the separate self-consciousness, "ceasing to draw a line around itself to divide itself from universal reality, will come to the absolute whole, not by advancing somewhither, but by abiding in that whereon the whole is based."

But there are heights above even the unity of intelligence; above the vision of an intelligence that is master of its faculties there is the intuition of an intelligence in love. Bereft of its faculties by the intoxication of the nectar, "it is reduced by love to that simple unity of being which is the perfect satisfaction of our souls." Of this final state of blessedness the soul has a foretaste and earnest here in moments of ecstasy.

We have seen how the soul may reascend to its source; but there is also a downward way, in which the soul may lose the dim consciousness of its origin which man retains, and thus sink to the level of the

SALVATION: RELIGION AND PHILOSOPHY 169

irrational animals or even to the purely vegetative life of plants.

Over against all these transcendental philosophies with their immaterial souls fallen from their high estate, incarcerated or entombed in fleshly bodies and subject to all the evils of this material world, the Stoics maintained a physical theology of immanence. The universe was permeated in every part and particle by a divine intelligence, purposeful and active, which was at the same time the all-pervasive energy that wrought all changes from within. This energetic intelligence, which is in the universe as the soul is in the body of man, they called Reason (Logos). The soul of man is of the same nature; it is in fact a particle of the universal soul, and is called by the same name, Logos. Neither in the world nor in man is the Logos immaterial—how could an immaterial anything move matter? It is itself merely the subtlest form of matter, which with the older physicists they recognized in heat, or "fire."

The well-being of man is founded in a life conformed to nature—the nature of man and the nature of the universe, which are the same. As the immanent divine reason is the ruling principle in the universe, so the human reason is the ruling faculty in man. To recognize this and to realize it by making reason constantly prevail over the impulses of the senses, the appetites and passions, is the meaning and end of the philosophic life.

The chief sphere of this endeavor is not to solve the metaphysical problems of the universe, but to live a wisely ordered life. Ethics is the culminating discipline of the Stoic system, to which logic and physics (of which theology is a subdivision) are subsidiary. The attainment is "virtue," which is the highest good, the only real good. As such it must be sought for its own sake—virtue is not virtue when it is made a means to anything else—and it is its own all-sufficing reward.

The later Stoicism, as we know it in the Roman period, became more theistic. Man not only imitated God by cultivating the same perfections, but communed in spirit with God, who is no remote being on the confines of the universe behind the outmost sphere, but is around us on every hand and within us. It was not in the temple and at the ear of the image that man conversed with God; God is a holy spirit dwelling in man's own soul.

To men who thought and felt thus; to whom bodily evils were no evils, but if rightly understood a divinely appointed discipline of character; to whom the whole ordering of life and history was a divine providence at once wise and good, salvation—if we may use that word—was a present progressive reality, and what was after death was of inferior concern. Whether the souls of the wise alone survived as individual souls; or whether all souls survived until the next world conflagration; or whether at death all souls returned into the universal soul of which they were but detached parts—on these points Stoic teachers were not agreed; but they would all have agreed in the words of Socrates: "No evil can befall a good man, either in life or death." The law of nature is the divine law of reason, and violation or neglect of it is revolt against nature, that is against God. Wrong-doing in this light assumes the character of sin, a conception of it to which the Stoics first gave full significance in ancient philosophy. Self-examination became an important part of the Stoic self-discipline; by it men sought to recognize and correct their faults.

As compared with the mysteries which offered themselves as ways of salvation by orgies and enthusiastic experiences or by initiations and sacraments, the superiority of these philosophies lay not alone in their rationality but even more in their essentially ethical character. They were in fact for centuries the religion of multitudes of high-minded men, who found in them not only the assurance of the hereafter but communion with God here and ideals and motives of human life. If such men were initiated into the mysteries, they found in the rites the ideas they brought with them and the experience they sought, as similar converts to Christianity interpreted its ἱερὸς λόγος, its teaching, and its sacraments (μυστήρια), in accord with their own thinking, and were furthered in it by them.

Christianity, after a long struggle, triumphed politically over the public religions of the Roman empire, and suppressed them. As a way of salvation it superseded all the mysteries and philosophies. Its success in this sphere is historically explained by the fact that catholic Christianity was a synthesis in which all the higher aspirations and endeavors of the Mediterranean area for long centuries was unified—the religious legacy of the ancient world to the ages that were to come. A word may therefore appropriately be said here in conclusion about this synthesis.

Christianity proclaimed itself among the Gentiles as a religion of the other world, in forms which must everywhere have been recognized as those of a mystery, and this aspect of its gospel has been greatly emphasized in recent times. It was, however, fundamentally different from the current mysteries.

SALVATION: RELIGION AND PHILOSOPHY 173

The mysteries, Greek or Oriental, concerned themselves solely with the other life; in principle they left this world and all its interests to the gods of the public religions, however initiates may have believed that a deity like Isis showed peculiar favor to her devotees in this life also. Nor had the mysteries any ethical character; they had in themselves no moral standards and no moral sanctions.

In Christianity, on the contrary, the fundamental article is faith in the one God, creator and ruler of heaven and earth, an omnipresent, omniscient, omnipotent God, who by his will orders all things in nature or history and whose providence comprehends every creature. He made man in his own image, endowed with reason and freedom, and requires of him conformity to his own character. He has implanted the moral law in the common conscience of mankind, and has made known his will more particularly by revelation in the Scriptures of the Old Testament. Neglect or transgression of this law is sin, and by this standard all men have sinned and come short of the glory of God. In his dealings with sinful men in this life God is just and merciful, and endeavors by the exhibition of both aspects of his character to bring men to repentance, that is, to a transformation of motive and a reformation of conduct—the dominance of love to God and love

to men, and the kind of life that springs from them.
God is perfectly good, and his end in all his relations
with men is their temporal and eternal well-being,
which in a moral universe is only possible through
righteousness and goodness.

Man is immortal, and character with its consequences endures beyond the tomb and there becomes
final. The judgment of God separates the righteous
and the wicked, the one to everlasting blessedness,
the other to misery.

All this is the direct inheritance of Christianity
from Judaism, and upon this foundation all the rest
is based. The Synagogue in the dispersion had
made the essentials of this theology widely known;
its ethical monotheism fell in with a strong current
of popular philosophy and commended it to many,
some of whom became proselytes, while a larger
number appropriated the ideas without formally
addicting themselves to the religion and being
naturalized in the Jewish people whose religion it
was.

The specific difference of Christianity is faith in
Jesus Christ. For the immediate disciples of Jesus
this meant the belief that he was the Messiah whom
the Jews had so long expected. His death was not
the refutation of this claim but the proof of it.
God had raised him from the dead and taken him

up to heaven, whence he was presently to come as the judge in the great assize, in which those who had rejected him, with all the wicked, would be condemned. The name Christianity, however, properly belongs to the form which this belief attained as it spread beyond the pale of Judaism. There the fundamental article of the distinctively Christian faith was that Jesus was not only the Messiah predicted in the prophets, but a supernatural being, a son of God, who came from heaven to suffer and die, and by his death and resurrection triumph over death, not for himself alone but for all who were united to him by faith, were initiated into his mystical body, the church, and participated in its sacraments. The affinity of these ideas to the mysteries is evident. Like them, also, Christianity was a way of salvation for all men, without distinction of race, condition, or religion—"Jew or Greek, barbarian, Scythian, bond or free."

But the differences are no less significant. In the mysteries the death of the Saviour was in itself meaningless—an incident of savage myth. The restoration to life, henceforth an immortal life, was the one essential thing, because the evil to be overcome, mortality, was a limitation of human nature which was transcended by participation in a divine nature. For Paul, on the contrary, to whom as a Jew the hindrance to a blessed hereafter under the moral government of God was sin, the death of Christ was an expiation for the sins of all mankind. But an even more fundamental difference is that in Christianity God himself is the author of salvation. In his limitless love to men he sent his Son from heaven to become man, to die for men's sins, and by his resurrection to open for them the way to eternal blessedness. A soteriology whose analogies are primarily un-Jewish was thus incorporated in a theology essentially Jewish, with the consequence, as we have seen in Paul's doctrine of redemption from sin, that the Christian salvation has an imperatively ethical character which is wholly foreign to the mysteries. But while in Judaism, as Paul represents it, righteousness according to the standard of the divine law is the indispensable—and impossible—condition of salvation, in Christianity a character conformed to God's own is the consequence of the grace of God in Jesus Christ, through the Holy Spirit. The possession of such a character is therefore the criterion of the genuineness of man's faith and the reality of his union with Christ.

The "Lord and Saviour Jesus Christ" was in the earliest Christology a divine being, the Son of God. Aside from the mythological misconceptions to which such a phrase was exposed, the conception itself seemed to collide with the emphatic monotheism which was the corner-stone of Christian faith, and this difficulty was greatly increased when, as immediately ensued, cosmic functions, including the creation of the world, were attributed to him. The effort to avoid this conflict in some of the epistles of Paul shows how soon the consciousness of it came. A somewhat similar problem had arisen in a different way in Hellenistic Judaism itself, and Philo had found a solution in the doctrine of the divine Logos. The beginnings of Christian philosophizing followed substantially the same line. Like Philo, their philosophy was a diluted Platonism, with Pythagorean leanings, and considerable appropriations from Stoicism not only on the ethical but on the theological side.

When Origen addressed himself to the construction of a system of Christian theology, or more exactly a speculative philosophy of the Christian religion, the philosophy was Platonism in the ultimate stage of its development as it has been described above in speaking of Plotinus. Though many things in Origen's imposing construction were rejected by the church as at variance with Scripture and tradition, as the whole system of his great predecessor Valentinus had been, Platonism remained what may be called the orthodox philosophy of the church, and this position was confirmed in the West by the great influence of Augustine.

Historical Christianity is therefore a cord of three strands, Jewish ethical monotheism; Hellenistic soteriology, profoundly modified by the Jewish element; and Greek philosophy, which not only constituted the formal principle of Christian theology but made large contributions to the material element. The ethical theism of Plato seemed to be the philosophical counterpart of the Jewish religious doctrine; and his conception of the way of salvation as conformation to the character of God, and of the goal as an eternal existence of the pure soul with God, was the sublimation of the doctrine of the mysteries. Christian mysticism was throughout Neoplatonic; the earliest compendium of Christian morals was based upon the ethics of the Stoic Panætius through Cicero's *De Officiis*.

The intellectual victory of Christianity over all the rival salvations of the time was due to the fact that it alone offered not merely a way of salvation but a philosophy of salvation.